1007449125

D0467716

159

HIRE
your first
EMPLOYEE

The entrepreneur's guide to finding, choosing and leading great people

Rhonda Abrams

thePlanning**shop**

The Planning Shop
Palo Alto, California

LIBRARY
GRANT MacEWAN
UNIVERSITY

Praise for Books from The Planning Shop

"User-friendly and exhaustive … highly recommended. Abrams' book works because she tirelessly researched the subject. Most how-to books on entrepreneurship aren't worth a dime; among the thousands of small business titles, Abrams' [is an] exception."

—*Forbes Magazine*

"Rhonda Abrams knows her target market. She did not try to be all things to all readers. This book is for people who want to be serious entrepreneurs … It comes down to the numbers … Rhonda Abrams makes sure you'll take care of the Bottom Line numbers."

—*Sean Murphy, Ernst & Young, LLP, New York*

"If you'd like something that goes beyond the mere construction of your plan and is more fun to use … this book can take the pain out of the process."

— *"Small Business School" (PBS television show)*

"This book stands head and shoulders above all others … and the perfect choice for the beginner and the experienced business professional."

—*BizCountry*

"It is my No. 1 recommendation to SBDC clients … I have always liked the layout, order of presentation, sidebar notes, and real-world perspective on the planning process, components of the plan, etc."

—*David Gay, Small Business Development Center, College of DuPage*

"I have to say—I reviewed several options on the Internet, and after much searching, ordered four different books that I thought would be the best to consider using in the course. The other three didn't even come close. This is a great book, especially for non-native speakers of English. Good work over there!"

—*Julie Carbajal, Fonty University of Applied Sciences, The Netherlands*

"You have done a great service in establishing your publishing company and in helping so many people to learn all the ins and outs of what can be a daunting experience. You've also saved people like me lots of money in the interim, as we learn and do what we can to realize our dreams."

—*S.M. Lourenco, VP, Imaginas, LLC, New York*

LIBRARY
GRANT MacEWAN
UNIVERSITY

"There are plenty of decent business-plan guides out there, but Abrams' was a cut above the others I saw. The Successful Business Plan won points with me because it was thorough and well organized, with handy worksheets and good quotes. Also, Abrams does a better job than most at explaining the business plan as a planning tool rather than a formulaic exercise. Well done."

—*Inc. Magazine*

"At last, a straightforward book that demystifies the process behind conducting effective business research ... gives business practitioners and students an incredibly useful tool to enable them to find accurate and timely information for business plans, academic papers, and other business uses."

—*Molly Lavik, Practitioner Faculty of Marketing, Graziadio School of Business and Management, Pepperdine University*

"I'm growing my business by purchasing a commercial building, and I needed a real estate loan to make the purchase. Business Plan In A Day was THE source I used for writing my plan, and the bankers and brokers I spoke with all commended my plan as being very strong and well written. Thanks to you, I've secured my loan and the transaction is going through. I feel so fortunate to have found this book."

—*Lisa Stillman, GardenWalk Massage Therapy, St. Louis*

"As a small business advisor, I use the Electronic Financial Worksheet (EFW) tool extensively in analyzing my clients' financials. I recommend the Planning Shop's EFW for any small business. It's the best cash flow financial planning tool on the market today."

—*Joe Lam, Certified Business Advisor, Texas State University Small Business Development Center*

"Your book has been both an inspirational read as well as a comprehensive guide. ... Being relatively inexperienced with entrepreneurship, your book has not only given me the ability to create a solid roadmap for planning, but has also provided an encouraging and easy way to cope with the enormous amount of information and organization needed."

—*Simon Lee, Entrepreneur*

"I just finished reading Rhonda's Trade Show In A Day and thought it was an excellent book and one that will stay close by my side during my next dozen shows. I highly recommend the book to anyone who wants to increase their productivity and profitability at their next trade event."

—*Gene Muchanski, President, Dive Industry Association*

Hire Your First Employee

©2010 by Rhonda Abrams. Published by The Planning Shop™

All rights reserved. No part of this publication may be reproduced, transmitted, stored in an information retrieval system, or used in any form or by any means, graphic, electronic, mechanical, photocopying, recording or otherwise, without the prior written permission of the publisher.

ISBN: 978-1-933895-13-0

Managing Editor: Rebecca Gaspar
Project Writers/Researchers: Mike McClary, Alice LaPlante
Project Researcher/Copyeditor: Anne Marie Bonneau
Cover Design: Diana Russell Design and Eric Powers
Interior Design: Diana Russell Design

Services for our readers

Colleges, business schools, corporate purchasing:
The Planning Shop offers special discounts and supplemental teaching materials for universities, business schools, and corporate training. Contact:

> info@PlanningShop.com
> or call 650-289-9120

Free business tips and information:
To receive The Planning Shop's free email newsletter on starting and growing a successful business, sign up at: www.PlanningShop.com.

> The Planning Shop™
> 555 Bryant Street, #180
> Palo Alto, CA 94301 USA
> 650-289-9120
>
> Fax: 650-289-9125
> Email: info@PlanningShop.com
> www.PlanningShop.com

The Planning Shop™ is a division of Rhonda, Inc., a California corporation.

Cover photograph of Rhonda Abrams by Garrett Hubbard
Interior photographs © istockphoto.com

"This publication is designed to provide accurate and authoritative information in regard to the subject matter covered. It is sold with the understanding that the publisher and author are not engaged in rendering legal, accounting, or other professional services. If legal advice or other expert assistance is required, seek the services of a competent professional."

— from a Declaration of Principles, jointly adopted by a committee o f the American Bar Association and a committee of publishers

Printed in Canada

10 9 8 7 6 5 4 3 2 1

About Rhonda Abrams

Entrepreneur, author, and nationally syndicated columnist Rhonda Abrams is widely recognized as one of the leading experts on entrepreneurship and small business. Rhonda's column for *USAToday*, "Successful Strategies," is the most widely distributed column on small business and entrepreneurship in the United States, reaching tens of millions of readers each week.

Rhonda's books have been used by millions of entrepreneurs. Her first book, *The Successful Business Plan: Secrets & Strategies,* is the best-selling business plan guide in America. It was named one of the Top Ten business books for entrepreneurs by both *Forbes* and *Inc.* magazines. She is also the author of more than a dozen other books on entrepreneurship and has sold more than a million copies of her books. Rhonda's other books are perennial best-sellers, with three of them having reached the nationally recognized "Top 50 Business Bestseller" list.

Rhonda not only writes about business—she lives it! As the founder of three successful companies, Rhonda has accumulated an extraordinary depth of experience and a real-life understanding of the challenges facing entrepreneurs. Rhonda first founded a management consulting practice working with clients ranging from one-person startups to Fortune 500 companies. Rhonda was an early Web pioneer, founding a website for small business that she later sold. In 1999, Rhonda started a publishing company—now called The Planning Shop—focusing exclusively on topics of business planning, entrepreneurship, and new business development. The Planning Shop is America's leading academic publisher focusing exclusively on entrepreneurship.

A popular public speaker, Rhonda is regularly invited to address leading industry and trade associations, business schools, and corporate conventions and events. Educated at Harvard University and UCLA, where she was named Outstanding Senior, Rhonda now lives in Palo Alto, California.

Register to receive Rhonda's free business newsletter at The Planning Shop's website, www.PlanningShop.com.

Other books by Rhonda Abrams include:

- *Successful Marketing: Secrets & Strategies*
- *The Successful Business Plan: Secrets & Strategies*
- *Six-Week Start-Up*
- *Business Plan In A Day*
- *The Owner's Manual for Small Business*
- *Successful Business Research*
- *What Business Should I Start?*
- *Winning Presentation In A Day*
- *Trade Show In A Day*
- *Wear Clean Underwear: Business Wisdom*
- *Finding an Angel Investor In A Day (Editor)*
- *Passion to Profits: Business Success for New Entrepreneurs*

About The Planning Shop

The Planning Shop specializes in creating business resources for entrepreneurs. The Planning Shop's books and other products are based on years of real-world experience, and they share secrets and strategies from entrepreneurs, CEOs, investors, lenders, and seasoned business experts. Products from The Planning Shop are known for their practical, honest advice and information, their easy-to-use format and worksheets, and their understanding of the real needs of businesspeople today.

Millions of entrepreneurs have used The Planning Shop's products to launch, run, and expand businesses in every industry. Since chief entrepreneur and CEO Rhonda Abrams founded The Planning Shop in 1999, more than 600 business schools, colleges, and universities have adopted The Planning Shop's books as required texts.

The Planning Shop's expanding line of business books includes:

- The *Successful Business* series, assisting entrepreneurs and business students in planning and growing businesses. Titles include *Successful Business Plan: Secrets & Strategies, Successful Marketing: Secrets & Strategies, Six-Week Start-Up, Successful Business Research, The Owner's Manual for Small Business*, and *What Business Should I Start?*

- The *In A Day* series, enabling entrepreneurs to tackle a critical business task and "Get it done right, get it done fast.™" Titles include *Business Plan In A Day, Winning Presentation In A Day, Trade Show In A Day, Finding an Angel Investor In A Day.*

- The *Better Business Bureau* series, helping entrepreneurs and consumers successfully make serious financial decisions. Titles include *Buying a Franchise, Buying a Home*, and *Starting an eBay Business.*

At The Planning Shop, now and in the future, you'll find the business information, books, and tools you need to make your business dreams a reality and your business plans a success. Learn more and register for our free business tips newsletter at *www.PlanningShop.com.*

Who This Book is for...

Do you want to grow your business? Starting a new business and need employees? Already have employees? This book is for you.

Hire Your First Employee: The entrepreneur's guide to finding, choosing, and leading great people is a complete, clear human resource handbook for the small business owner or manager. It's designed for entrepreneurs who are:

- Starting a new business and need employees from day one: businesses like retail stores, hospitality industry, restaurants, software developers, construction industry

- Solo entrepreneurs with a growing business and need someone to help, whether with administrative tasks or with core business skills, whether on a contract basis or as an employee

- Professional consultants or skilled workers spending time on administrative tasks instead of income-producing activities

- Existing businesses using part-time workers, contractors and considering converting some of these to regular employees

- Existing businesses with employees but needing to set up better systems to handle the paperwork, develop personnel policies, improve your management skills

Hire Your First Employee: The entrepreneur's guide to finding, choosing, and leading great people provides you with all the fundamental information you need to make informed, better choices about issues such as:

- how much to pay and how much you can afford

- what jobs to hire for first

- what benefits and policies to adopt

- health, dental and vision insurance, retirement plans, and more

- whether to hire employees or contractors, full-time or part-time

- how to stay well within the law

- what taxes and paperwork you're responsible for

- how to easily handle payroll

- how to find the best job candidates

- what questions to ask—and not to ask—in interviews

- how to become a better leader and manager

- how to get the most from your employees

Hire Your First Employee: The entrepreneur's guide to finding, choosing, and leading great people doesn't just give you **information,** it also gives you **advice.** This guide shows you what other small businesses do and what you can do, must do, and most do.

As you go through this guide, you'll find dozens of **Worksheets,** so by the time you go through this book, you'll have your own set of plans, procedures and policies.

If you have employees and own a small business, this book is for you!

Contents

Section One: Making the Decision to Hire   3

CHAPTER 1   The Time is Right to Hire!   4

Benefits of Hiring Employees   6

Bad Economy, Good Time for Hiring   7

Envisioning the Growth of Your Business   9

The Ultimate Social Responsibility   9

worksheet: Goals for Growing My Business   10

CHAPTER 2   Scope Out Your Specific Needs   12

What Role for Your New Hire?   12

worksheet: Business Tasks   14

Help Wanted, But How Much?   15

worksheet: Employee Tasks   16

worksheet: Who Do I Need on My Team?   18

How Much Can You Afford?   20

worksheet: How Much Can I Afford?   21

success story: Successful Cheese Maker Hires for Skill Sets She Lacks   22

Logistics   23

worksheet: Logistics   24

Section Two: The Nitty Gritty—Employee Status, Labor Laws, Payroll and Taxes 27

CHAPTER 3   Understanding Employee Status 28

Determining Your Worker's Status 28

success story: Hanna Design Limited 37

CHAPTER 4   Employment and Labor Law—The Basics 38

Key Labor Laws 39

worksheet: Employment Laws as They Apply to Me 45

CHAPTER 5   Managing Payroll and Payroll Taxes 46

Payroll Basics 46

Payroll Taxes 54

Options for Managing Payroll 56

worksheet: Choosing a Payroll Service 58

Entering Payroll Data and Payroll Reports 60

Section Three: Your Policies, Benefits and Company Culture *67*

CHAPTER 6   What Should I Pay My New Employee? *68*

Researching Comparable Pay Rates *69*

worksheet: My Compensation Research *70*

Salary, Hourly, Commission, Tips? *72*

success story: Custom Product for Auto Industry Developed with Equity Offer to Family & Friends *74*

worksheet: Calculate Sales Commission *75*

worksheet: Estimate My Labor Costs *76*

The Bottom Line *77*

CHAPTER 7   Design Your Benefits Plan *78*

What Benefits to Offer? *78*

Health Insurance *80*

worksheet: Health Care Questions to Ask Yourself *85*

Choosing a Healthcare Plan *86*

Other Paid Benefits *86*

Get Creative with Benefits *89*

worksheet: Questions to Ask Insurance Companies/Agents *90*

worksheet: Dental Insurance Plans *92*

worksheet: Explore Your Health Care Options *94*

CHAPTER 8 **Paid Time Off, Personnel Policies, and Your Company Culture** *96*

Time Off—Paid and Unpaid *97*

worksheet: Sick Leave *99*

worksheet: Vacation Policy *101*

worksheet: Holiday Policy *103*

worksheet: Personal and other Leave *105*

success story: Accounting Firm Sees Value in Creative Benefits Package *107*

Attendance, Work Hours, Time Tracking, Telecommuting *108*

worksheet: Unpaid Time Off *109*

worksheet: Work Hours Policies *111*

Expenses and Reimbursements *112*

worksheet: Reimbursement Policies *113*

Personal Conduct *114*

worksheet: Personal Conduct *115*

Your Company Culture: What Do You Stand For? *116*

Section Four: Finding and Hiring the Right People   119

CHAPTER 9   The Search is On—Finding Applicants   120

Write a Powerful Job Description   120

sample document: Sample Job Description   122

worksheet: Write a Job Description   123

Craft a Compelling Help Wanted Ad   124

sample document: Two Approaches to a Help Wanted Ad   126

worksheet: Plan Your Want Ad   127

Choose the Perfect Place for Your Ad   128

The Application Process   130

success story: Sub Shop Owner Finds Sweet Spot with Part-Timers   131

sample document: Employment Application Form   132

CHAPTER 10   Interviewing   134

Review Resumes for Winners   134

Effective Phone Screening   136

worksheet: Phone-Interview Questionnaire/Notes   137

In-Person Interviews That Click   138

success story: Cultural Fit Comes First at Growing Tech Company   140

CHAPTER 11   Making the Offer and Negotiating   144

Evaluate Your Candidates   145

worksheet: Candidate Evaluation Form   146

Check References & Backgrounds   147

Making the Offer   148

sample document: Offer Letter   149

sample document: Drug Screen Authorization Letter   151

sample document: Credit Report Authorization   151

sample document: Rejection Letter   153

Section Five: The First Day and Beyond *155*

CHAPTER 12   Day One: Start off Strong   *156*

Welcome Aboard!   *156*

sample document: Employee Introduction Email   *158*

worksheet: My Preparation for Day One   *159*

sample document: Sample Day One Agenda   *160*

Day One Training   *161*

worksheet: Day One Checklist   *162*

CHAPTER 13   Becoming the Boss   *164*

You're the Boss: Leader or Manager?   *164*

worksheet: Management Traits   *167*

Motivating and Retaining Employees   *170*

Lead by example   *172*

Performance Review: 30 Days and Beyond   *173*

Letting Employees Go   *173*

worksheet: Employee Action Plan for Improving Performance   *174*

Look Who's The Boss   *175*

worksheet: Employee Performance Evaluation   *176*

Section One:
Making the Decision to Hire

CHAPTER 1   *The Time is Right to Hire* 4

CHAPTER 2   *Scope Out Your Specific Needs* 12

chapter 1

The Time is Right to Hire!

" Never doubt that a small group of thoughtful, committed citizens can change the world. Indeed, it is the only thing that ever has. "
—MARGARET MEAD

It's true. Few things make such a difference in your own business, your life, the life of others and the economy as a whole as when you hire an employee. It's almost impossible to grow a company of any size and worth unless you expand beyond yourself. If you want to grow your business, at some point, you'll have to decide how and when to bring others on board.

Hiring an employee—even a part-timer—can enrich your experience as a business owner and lead you toward personal and financial growth. Let's face it—until you hire someone else, even if you're self-employed, you've basically created a job for yourself. That means that when you stop working—even for an hour—you've stopped making money. When you hire someone else, you're creating a business. If you structure it correctly, you can make money when others work.

What's more, by hiring someone to assist with your business and treating them well and fairly, you're providing a valuable, respectable job for someone, enabling them to support themselves and their family. It's one of the most satisfying, rewarding things that you, as a businessperson, can do. Sure, there are challenges. But when you create a good job for someone, you've changed the world for the better.

Hiring is a big step. It involves a lot more than just a desire to grow. But if you plan carefully, select the right people, and learn basic skills on how to be a good boss, you'll be on your way to higher income, greater satisfaction, and a successful, healthy business.

More customers. More sales. Less grunt work. A healthier economy. Creating good jobs for others. A re-energized you. Add it up and you'll see why hiring your first employees can lead to a new wave of growth for your business and more satisfaction in your life.

Of course, you're ready to make the decision to hire—that's why you've picked up this book. You know you need staff to get your business launched, to handle the demands of your burgeoning business, or to augment the talents or skills you lack.

But you're also a bit spooked by all the other stuff that comes when you have employees, things such as:

- Deciding what responsibilities to give to your new employee

- Figuring out how much to pay and how much you can afford

- Finding, interviewing and selecting the best person for the job

- What benefits and personnel policies you should adopt

- Following and understanding employment and other labor laws

- Dealing with the paperwork and payroll

- Managing and leading others, becoming a boss

That's where this book comes in. It will guide you—clearly—through all the basics of what you need to know to find, hire, pay, manage, lead employees and stay well within the law.

Becoming a Boss

Especially if you're managing people for the first time, you need to start thinking of what type of boss you want to be.

Let's be frank: You're not going to learn to be a great boss, leader and manager over night or from just a book. It takes time. It takes experience. And it takes a commitment to learning the skills and attitudes to manage and lead others. That's an ongoing process.

When to Make the Leap

It's time to hire if you:

☐ Need employees on Day One of your business

☐ Turn away work from new or current clients because you're over-booked

☐ Can't find time to send invoices to your customers

☐ Can't get out from under your paperwork

☐ Lack time to pursue new product ideas and/or new clients

☐ Need someone with specialized skills critical to your business

☐ Want to grow a business you can sell one day

Having Employees Enables You To...

- Serve more customers.
- Produce more products or services.
- Add additional skills & talents to your business.
- Spend your time on more money-producing activities.
- Use your time on the things you do best and like to do.
- Make money when someone else is working.
- Grow your company.

Benefits of Hiring Employees

Grow Your Business

Hiring an employee helps you be more productive. You have more time to focus on growth—to develop innovative new products, reach out to your customers, spend less time on administrative tasks, or simply focus more energy on your work.

- Concentrate on the work you do best
- Increase your sales
- Manage more customers
- Balance your weaknesses
- Create a business that you might eventually be able to sell to others

Change Your Life

Working alone can be lonely. It's hard to make all the decisions by yourself, stay motivated, handle all the day-to-day tasks of running even a very small business. Having someone else on board brings you more talent and skills.

- Share some of your workload
- Spend more of your time on work you enjoy
- Reduce isolation
- Turn to someone else; bounce ideas off of them
- Recharge your battery

Change the World

In 2007, there were 21 million businesses in the US with NO employees. Some will never have the income to support employees. But if a mere 1% of those businesses hired just one employee, they'd create 200,000 new jobs! You can be part of that.

- Create good jobs for other people
- Create an atmosphere in which people are treated fairly and with respect
- Increase employment in America and reduce unemployment
- Improve the economy

But this book definitely helps you get started. You'll be armed with enough of the basic knowledge you need as an employer. You'll get the guidance to help you conduct an effective hiring search that should result in finding a great employee. You'll feel more confident that you understand the laws and day-to-day processes of dealing with employees. You'll think through your company's policies and benefits and what kind of corporate culture you want to cultivate. Finally, you'll take a look at managing and leading your staff. You'll be on your way to charting a path toward another successful chapter in your business' story.

Bad Economy, Good Time for Hiring

Weak economy? High unemployment? Sure, it's scary to think about expanding your business and taking on employees during uncertain economic conditions. But believe it or not, recessions and depressions have historically proven to be great times to start or grow a business. And a time of high unemployment may be the very best time to add to your staff.

More than half of all companies that make up the Fortune 500 or Dow Industrial Average were started in a recession or depression. Statistically speaking, you've got a better chance of becoming a huge American corporation by starting in a bad economy.

Take a look at some of the companies that started or expanded substantially during recessions or depressions: Microsoft, McDonalds, Disney, Hewlett-Packard, Whole Foods, General Electric, Adobe, J.Crew, Intuit, Alcoa, Johnson & Johnson, Procter & Gamble, Applebees, Costco, Chilis, Odwalla, Sara Lee, Sears. The list goes on and on.

HIRELearning

Small Businesses:

- Generate more than 45 percent of total private payroll
- Create 60 to 80 percent of new jobs annually
- Employ half of all private-sector employees
- Hire 40 percent of all technology workers

—Small Business Administration

Yes, it seems counter-intuitive, but it's actually not a fluke. Bad economic times mean great opportunities for companies willing to expand, be aggressive, and take risks. That's because you'll find:

- **Weaker competition.** In bad economic times, big companies tighten their belts, cutting back on marketing, new product introductions, research and development, expansion. That makes it a better time for smaller, more aggressive competitors—like you!

- **More flexible customers.** In good economies, customers don't switch providers much. But when times get bad, they look for new, better, cheaper alternatives. They're far more open to trying new things and new companies.

- **Lower costs and better terms.** Suppliers are more willing to deal during bad economies. In fact, in good times, many suppliers won't even deal with new, small companies.

- **Lower rents.** If you need expanded space to accommodate your new employees or launch your new business, you'll find all types of commercial real estate less expensive—office, retail, warehouse, manufacturing space.

Debunking Hiring Myths

MYTH	REALITY
Hiring an employee costs too much money.	Your income is limited if you work only by yourself. Hire smart and your new help enables you to make more money.
I must offer employees a whole range of costly benefits.	Legally, the number of benefits you must offer is surprisingly small. However, you'll probably choose to offer more to get the best employees.
I'll have to pay payroll taxes as well as salary or wages.	That's true. Budget for these as you plan. And when legal, you can use independent contractors without paying taxes.
I don't have enough money saved up to hire full-time employees.	You can start small—hiring part-time workers or contractors.
I don't have enough space in my office for an employee.	Many businesses can have employees who telecommute at least part of the time.
I'll spend all my time on paperwork, managing payroll, and figuring taxes.	A wealth of services, like online payroll, help you handle these quickly and easily.
Managing other people will take up too much of my time.	Once you get systems in place, you should have more time for doing work you're best at.
Employees are lazy, more trouble than they're worth.	Most people are eager to do a good job. Train them well and manage fairly, and they'll work hard for you.

High Unemployment = Lots of Great Prospects

Frankly, when unemployment is high, it's a buyer's market for those hiring. You'll find better workers, at lower cost, willing to be more flexible.

Certainly, a job loss is devastating to the people who are laid off. However, this means that some of the most skilled workers are available to help you take your business to the next level. And although it's awful when recent college graduates can't find good jobs, that means there are lots of eager, smart, young people you can add to your team.

Times of high unemployment offers employers:

- **Cheaper labor.** Prospects recognize they may have to take lower wages or salaries to get a job.

- **Talented employees.** In good times, it's often hard for small companies to compete against big corporations for the best people. In bad times, even highly talented, experienced employees are willing to work for small companies, or have been laid off from corporate positions, bringing unmatched experience to you.

- **Flexible workers.** Job prospects are more willing to work around your needs and schedule, including being more open to part-time work or off-hours.

- **Greater choice of independent contractors.** Just as more prospects are willing to work part-time, you'll find a large pool of talented people willing to work as independent contractors, exploring self-employment or making money until they find another full-time job.

■ **Experienced retirees.** Recessionary conditions mean many workers accepted "early retirement" packages, while other retirees have seen their retirement savings and investments decline. This means many more experienced workers are looking for part-time or full-time roles to use the skills they've gained over a lifetime.

Even if your dream isn't to start a multi-billion enterprise, history shows that if large, long-standing corporations can take-off during a challenging economy, your company can too!

Envisioning the Growth of Your Business

Before you begin the hiring process, you need to begin to make the "mental leap" to this next stage of your business. Perhaps you've been a "solo-preneur," working on your own, maybe basing your business from your home. Hiring someone will make a major change in your lifestyle as well as your business. Perhaps you're starting the type of business that requires one or more employees right off the bat, such as a restaurant, store, or manufacturing plant. Besides building a business, you also have to build your skills as "boss"—spending part of your time managing and leading employees.

Where do you see your business in a year? Three years? Five years? How does having employees or other workers help you achieve your goals? Think about adding employees within the context of your larger business goals.

Use the worksheet "Goals for Growing My Business" to consider what you want your business to look like in the next few years. That gives you a context for deciding what type of employees to hire and how soon.

The fact is, adding an employee to your business is one of the most powerful methods for bringing in more work from new and existing customers, delivering a higher level of service or giving yourself the time to brainstorm innovative new products and services. In other words, you *can* hire your way to growth.

The Ultimate Social Responsibility

Many entrepreneurs hope that their businesses will have a positive impact on society—that their companies will not only make a profit but help to make the world a better place. They've identified a product or service that people need or want and hope to fill that void. Most care about their communities, the environment, helping reduce poverty. But few people talk about the tremendous positive impact that creating a good job has on society as a whole. And how satisfying it truly is—if you allow yourself to recognize the importance of creating jobs.

The ultimate act of social responsibility is to create a job—a good job—and then to treat your employees fairly and decently. Think about this for a moment: did you ever have a job where they paid you a good, competitive wage, in a work environment where people were given respect and thanked when they did a good job? Where you had a chance to have your ideas listened to, where there was no discrimination or bias? If you did, you know what a wonderful difference it made in your life. Every day you had a chance to spend your hours in a positive environment—even if you had to work hard. If you didn't—and most people don't—then you can imagine how wonderful such a work environment like that would be.

You—as an employer—have the opportunity to create that kind of situation for others. And that's an incredibly important contribution to the world. That doesn't mean you can't be a demanding boss—you can indeed demand hard work and high standards. But if you can create a job, pay fair wages and benefits, respect and acknowledge your employees, and create an environment of fairness and acceptance, you can go to sleep at night—every night—knowing that you have changed the lives of others for the better. And they, in turn, will change yours.

worksheet: Goals for Growing My Business

Specific Goals:

Enter the number or amount you hope to achieve for your business in one year, five years, and ten years.

	One Year	Five Years	Ten Years
Number of Employees	_____	_____	_____
Number of Locations	_____	_____	_____
Annual Sales	_____	_____	_____
Profits or Profit Margin	_____	_____	_____
Number of Products/Services	_____	_____	_____
Awards/Recognition Received	_____	_____	_____
Ownership Allocation	_____	_____	_____
Other:	_____	_____	_____

Priorities:

Rate your priorities for your business.

	Urgent	Important	I'll get to it sooner or later	Not on the radar screen	Not applicable to my business
Add Employees	☐	☐	☐	☐	☐
Add New Lines	☐	☐	☐	☐	☐
Increase Marketing	☐	☐	☐	☐	☐
Add Locations	☐	☐	☐	☐	☐
Expand Online	☐	☐	☐	☐	☐
Increase Salaries	☐	☐	☐	☐	☐
Increase Inventory	☐	☐	☐	☐	☐
Increase Profits	☐	☐	☐	☐	☐
Retire Debts	☐	☐	☐	☐	☐
Increase Reserve	☐	☐	☐	☐	☐
Acquire Other Companies	☐	☐	☐	☐	☐

Other:

_____	☐	☐	☐	☐	☐
_____	☐	☐	☐	☐	☐
_____	☐	☐	☐	☐	☐
_____	☐	☐	☐	☐	☐
_____	☐	☐	☐	☐	☐
_____	☐	☐	☐	☐	☐
_____	☐	☐	☐	☐	☐
_____	☐	☐	☐	☐	☐

2

Scope Out Your Specific Needs

The way a team plays as a whole determines its success. You may have the greatest bunch of individual stars in the world, but if they don't play together, the club won't be worth a dime.
—BABE RUTH

You know you need help, and you're ready to take the step to hiring someone. Whoa! Before you run your first help wanted ad, you need to figure out a few things: what will your employee be doing, where will you put them, and can you afford to pay them and still have money to pay all your other bills and yourself too?

Doing a bit of background work prepares you for the process of finding and hiring a great employee. You'll find you're much more confident about every aspect of becoming a boss when you're sure about what you need an employee to do, you've determined that you can afford to hire them, and you've considered the basic logistics of having someone else around to share the day-to-day responsibilities of your business.

What Role for Your New Hire?

First things first: What, exactly, do you need an employee to do? Clarifying—at first for yourself and later for your employee—the tasks and responsibilities you'll want them to tackle sets the foundation for a job description you'll develop soon (see Chapter 9 on Finding Applicants).

But before you can do that, on a simpler level, you have to spend some time identifying your goals and envisioning your new employee's role and responsibilities. What will they work on? What tasks do you most want them to accomplish? How will they help your business succeed and grow? The more clearly you define the work you want them to do and the role you envision them filling, the more likely you are to find a candidate who's an appropriate fit for your needs.

One of the most important things to examine is which roles you want to keep for yourself and which you'd rather assign to others. Which items on your crowded plate should you delegate to an employee and which do you want or need to keep yourself?

Let's say you own a one-person hair salon, and you're fully booked with appointments. But you're frazzled. You have to carve time out of your day for scheduling, ordering supplies, and shampooing customers.

You're ready for growth and you have a couple options regarding what type of employee to hire:

1. **A receptionist/assistant.** Someone to do the support work allows you to concentrate on customers and earn more per hour on doing what you love—styling hair. They can answer the phone, shampoo waiting customers, clean and order supplies. The downside: they don't bring in direct, additional income.

2. **A second hairdresser.** They'll bring in new customers, more income, and help your top line to grow. The downside: they don't free you up from the stuff you don't like to do. In fact, you may spend more time answering phones.

Most businesspeople face similar dilemmas when choosing what type of employee to hire. The choices frequently boil down to: hiring someone to help you take care of administrative or basic operations of your business, freeing your time for more lucrative activities OR hiring a salesperson to bring in more customers OR adding someone who does the same/similar tasks as you and who'll, hopefully, bring in more money.

Of course, for certain types of businesses, the kinds of employees you'll need will be fairly obvious. Starting a restaurant, for example, you know you need a chef/cook, wait staff, and bussers. You may need a host or cashier. But even then, you'll want to take a look at which of these jobs—if any—you'll choose to perform yourself and which you'll hire others to do. Perhaps you want to be the cook or the host. It's a good idea to sit down and figure out which jobs you want.

Typically, for most small businesses, the first hires fall into one of these categories:

- Administrative
- Bookkeeping
- Sales
- Production/service workers

Use the worksheet "Business Tasks" to brainstorm about the jobs you need done in your business. You will likely produce a fairly long list. Don't worry. After compiling your list, indicate whether you want to keep these tasks for yourself, hand them over to someone else, or share these duties. This will start to give you an idea of the jobs you'd like to hire others to complete.

As you jot down your ideas, be aware of the two biggest mistakes business owners make when hiring an employee:

1. Handing over *too much* authority

2. Not giving over *any* authority

Recognize that you have to relinquish some control if you want your business to grow, and your employee to be effective and satisfied.

You're almost certain to have a long, long list of things you'd like someone else to do. Prioritize what you'd like accomplished.

Can they all be undertaken by the same person? In a small business, it's typical for people to wear many hats, but you still have to consider whether one real-live person can manage very different tasks. For instance, is it realistic to imagine that the person who handles your administrative paperwork can also do some basic bookkeeping, shipping, and some basic work on your website? Probably. But is it realistic to think the person who's going to handle your administrative tasks can also manage your computer network, handle your back-end technology needs, and make sales calls? Probably not.

worksheet: **Business Tasks**

List—as much as possible—the tasks you need done in your business. Identify which ones you want to keep entirely for yourself, which you'd like to hand over to an employee (or other help) and which tasks you'll share.

TASK	KEEP MYSELF	DELEGATE	SHARE

Also, don't be surprised if you end up in a different place than you expected. Maybe at first you just *knew* you needed a sales person only to discover that an administrative assistant makes more sense.

Use the Worksheet, "Employee Tasks" to list the kinds of jobs you want your new employee to handle, what background they need to accomplish those tasks, and how many hours a week you expect them to devote to those tasks.

Help Wanted, But How Much?

Now that you've decided what position you should fill first, you need to consider how much time you'll require from an employee. Do you need a full-time worker? A part-timer? A contractor or consultant? Based on your job requirements—and your budget—consider the range of your options for getting the help you need:

- **Full-time employees.** This is just what it sounds like: you hire individuals to work for you, devoting between 30-40 hours a week (or more), usually five days a week. Full-time workers can be salaried employees or paid hourly. Because they work for you full-time, you know you have their time, skills and attention when you need it.

- **Part-time employees.** It's very likely that you'll have certain functions that don't require a full-time employee. Let's say you only need an administrative assistant a few hours each day or you need help in your bed & breakfast on the weekends. You may even be able to find part-time employees for some professional tasks, such as marketing, managing technology, or bookkeeping. Utilizing part-time employees saves money, but they may be tempted to look for full-time work elsewhere. Generally, part-time workers are paid by the hour. They are still covered by all employment laws.

- **Independent contractors.** Before you ever hire an employee, it's likely you'll get help by engaging an independent contractor. Independent contractors are individuals who perform specific tasks, generally for a limited period of time. Most often they're used for professional tasks, such as accounting, marketing, or tech help. Using an independent contractor offers many advantages—most notably, you're not responsible for payroll taxes and they're not covered by labor laws. You also control costs because you only pay for the time you actually use them. And you can cut back on their services rapidly if they're no longer needed. But the government carefully limits the use of independent contractors, and you can get in big trouble if you don't follow the law (see Chapter 3 on Employee Status).

- **Interns.** Interns are usually students or other individuals just starting out in a profession who are eager to learn the ropes and are willing to work for minimum wage (or even for free—but only if they receive college credit and are doing meaningful work) to gain much-needed experience. Working with interns is a great way to get inexpensive help in your business while also getting fresh ideas from a younger audience. However, interns are very inexperienced, require significant supervision time, and leave quickly.

HIRELearning

A Part-Timer in Your Future?

Small businesses with 1 to 24 employees hire a quarter of their employees on a part-time basis. In businesses with more than 100 employees, part-timers make up only about 14 percent of the workforce.

—Small Business Administration

worksheet: **Employee Tasks**

Use this worksheet to capture the tasks you need to accomplish to run your business, the skills required, then add up the amount of time each will take.

TASKS TO ACCOMPLISH	SKILLS, EDUCATION AND EXPERIENCE REQUIRED	HOURS PER WEEK
	TOTAL:	

Also, consider whether the employee will be:

- **Permanent.** Most employees are hired on a permanent basis. This doesn't mean that they have life-time employment (you want to make certain they know they're hired on an "at will basis"—see Chapter 3 on Employee Status). But it does mean that the length of time of their employment is open-ended; you both expect it to continue.

- **Temporary.** Many companies are seasonal, and you may only need employees during your busy times. You can hire full or part-time employees on a temporary basis. You are still responsible for payroll taxes, and your temporary employees are still covered by federal and state employment laws. If you have a short-term project (perhaps for a few months) that you must staff up for, you can hire temporary employees or use consultants.

With a clear understanding of the tasks and responsibilities you have in mind for your new employee, you can decide what level of support you need. Stay open to evaluating your needs and options. You might be convinced you need a full-time person, only to find that you'd be better off with a part-time person and a consultant.

If you're growing fast or opening a company that needs a lot of help from the starting gate, it's likely you'll need a mix of full-time and part-time people. If you're launching a new software company, for example, you might decide you can do sales while you hire a full-time engineer, a part-time administrative assistant, and some additional contractors for writing code. You might even get an intern to do some research for you.

Deciding How Much Help You Need

EMPLOYEE TYPE	ADVANTAGES	DISADVANTAGES	PAYROLL TAXES?	QUICK TIPS
Full-time	Larger labor pool to choose from; more staff stability; increased attention and loyalty; lower employee turnover	More expensive; less flexibility; higher benefits costs	Yes	30-40 hours per week generally constitutes full-time status
Part-time	Lower cost; greater flexibility; typically fewer benefits; you still have direct supervision	Likely increased turnover; harder to find professional/skilled staff; lower staff satisfaction	Yes	You pay the same percentage In employment taxes for part-time as full-time employees
Independent Contractor	No employment taxes; great flexibility; experienced workers; no cost when not utilizing	Higher per hour cost; may not be able to get them when you need them; not under your supervision	No	Make certain you are following all IRS rules or face stiff penalties
Intern	May be able to work for free if they get college credit; low cost; often eager and smart	Inexperienced, need considerable supervision, inconsistent work standards, quick turnover	If paid, yes	You must pay interns at least minimum wage unless they are receiving school credit for their work

worksheet: Who Do I Need on My Team?

List the job titles needed in each area. Some suggestions are in parentheses, but you should hire only those your company really needs as it grows.

KEY PERSONNEL	RESPONSIBILITIES	DESIRED EXPERIENCE/ BACKGROUND
Top Management (President/CEO)		
Administrative (Office Manager, Administrative Assistants)		
Financial (Controller, bookkeeper, etc.)		
Marketing/Sales/PR (VP Marketing, Salesperson, PR Director)		
Operations/Production (Production Manager)		
Technology (Chief Technology Officer, Website developer, tech support staff)		
Human Resources (Personnel Director)		
Logistics Staff (Shipping clerk, janitor)		
Other		

DESIRED ATTITUDES/ HABITS	DESIRED EDUCATION/ TRAINING	SKILLS NEEDED	COMPENSATION

Hiring an employee helps you grow your business, especially if you've carefully considered what type of employee you need and how much you can afford. Having another person onboard gives you more time to focus on growth—to develop innovative new products, reach out to your customers, spend less time on administrative tasks, or simply focus more energy on your work.

How Much Can You Afford?

One of the biggest hurdles to overcome when deciding to hire is figuring out how much you can afford. You're probably, naturally, worried about how you'll afford to pay an employee *and* still have enough income for yourself. After all, if you don't make enough money in a month, you still have to pay your employees—it's the law. That means you might not have enough money to pay for other things—your rent, your suppliers, yourself.

Fear over making enough money is probably the biggest obstacle to becoming an employer. But employees are an investment in your business—not just a cost—and the goal is greater growth. As with every investment, you can address your concerns with some careful planning.

When figuring out how much you can pay an employee, take the following steps:

1. **Review your current monthly cash flow.** How much money goes through your business each month? Remember, even if your business is profitable at the end of the year, you have to make payroll every two weeks or so. That means you need cash in the bank. So be sure to first take a realistic look at your monthly dollars in and dollars out.

2. **Estimate your current monthly profit.** Have you consistently been generating enough income to support the type of employee you need, as well as yourself?

HIRELearning

Figuring Taxes and Benefits

While you're considering how much you can afford for a new employee, remember to also budget for payroll taxes and benefits. As a rule of thumb, budget 15-30% of their salary for additional expenses.

3. **Estimate expected additional income.** The goal of hiring employees is to enable you to make more money. How much will your new employee realistically help you generate? In what time frame? Be conservative in these projections, especially at first.

4. **Estimate how much you'll have to pay an employee.** You need to know how much you'll have to budget for your employee(s). Once you decide what role and tasks you want your new employee to assume, determine comparable pay rates (see Chapter 6).

5. **Estimate monthly taxes and benefits.** Don't forget that you also have to pay taxes and benefits. The total amount will depend on which benefits you decide to offer.

6. **Estimate additional costs.** Having employees means you typically have other additional costs. Will you pay higher rent for more space? Have increased telecom, travel, or energy expenses? Even greater use of office equipment? Make a guesstimate of some of these costs as well.

A good plan is to save up for payroll, just as you save for other investments. Set up a separate payroll account with enough money to cover at least three months worth of payroll and taxes. Expect to make payroll from monthly cash flow rather than this separate account, which acts as an emergency back-up in case you have a bad month. This financial cushion allows you to hire with more confidence.

worksheet: How Much Can I Afford?

Use this worksheet to estimate how much money you'll have available each month to go towards wages/salaries.

A. Current monthly profit	
B. Estimated increased monthly income	
C. Subtotal: Add (A) profit and (B) increased income	
D. Expected monthly salary/wages	
E. Estimated monthly taxes/benefits	
F. Estimated other monthly costs	
G. Subtotal: Add (D)wages, (E) taxes/benefits and (F) other costs	
TOTAL: Subtract line G from line C.	

SUCCESS STORY

Successful Cheese Maker
Hires for Skill Sets She Lacks

In the early '80s, Mary Keehn, a breeder of Alpine goats along the foggy Northern California coast, began to dabble in cheese making using milk from her herd. By 1983, she was ready to transform her business from raising goats to creating fine cheeses made from goat's milk. Cypress Grove was born. Housed first in her home and later in a small creamery, Keehn started small. For two years, she employed just a part-timer to ladle cheese, clean up between batches, and take care of anything else necessary. Then, as goat cheese increased in popularity in the U.S., Keehn needed more help. "I hired people here and there as I needed them, not with any grand plan. I hired out of necessity," she says.

Keehn brought aboard people who had skills in areas she did not, such as accounting. For that, she looked in-house for help literally. "When she was in high school, my oldest daughter did the books as a school project," she says. All four of Keehn's daughters worked in the business. "I think it's important in a family business that everyone be involved to some degree. I enjoyed having my daughters work here when they were young. I always knew where they were – and knew they were safe!"

As the company continued to grow, Keehn, recognizing the importance of hiring for attitude, brought on board good people and trained them to do what was needed. "When we hire someone, we pay attention to them, to how they work, and to their capacity for taking on more responsibility," she says. "If you push

people, they'll leave. But by paying attention to what they can do, you can see the person grow with the business."

By the time Cypress Grove had a staff of ten, the creamery became cramped. "We worked in our first creamery until we were stepping on each other's toes," Keehn says. "But we weren't ready to move into a larger space yet so we scheduled split shifts and did other things to help the situation. You can always work it out if you get creative."

Despite her hiring successes, Keehn says she regrets not filling one particular role sooner: a seasoned operations manager. "It was the best hire I've made but also the one that took the longest," she says. "When I was just starting the business, I knew I could benefit from someone with an operations background, but I honestly didn't think I could afford it." After years of managing the day-to-day business, Keehn found it difficult to hand over responsibility to someone. "If an operations or management person is good, they need autonomy or they won't be successful and neither will the business."

Keehn's staffing method—first hire part-time help, ask for support from family members, but then tap the expertise of established business people—has paid off. More than a quarter-century since selling its first cheeses as a two-person enterprise, today Cypress Grove employs a staff of nearly fifty. Their cheeses, including Humboldt Fog, have won an impressive array of awards, including first place from the American Cheese Society and three World Cheese Award gold medals.

To get used to becoming an employer, you might want to start slowly: hire part-time workers or contractors and track your expenses. See whether you're confidently able to make payroll. If the kind of help you need can legally be fulfilled by independent contractors, get used to the financial burden by first hiring contractors rather than employees. That will give you an idea of whether you can manage the cash flow without worrying about having to lay someone off if the budget is too tight.

Logistics

As you think about adding an employee or employees, there's a whole bunch of logistical nitty-gritty details that are probably also on your mind, such as where they'll work, their work hours, even where they'll put their stuff.

So take a bit of time to work out the basic logistical aspects of having an employee. And don't worry: most of these details become fairly obvious pretty quickly.

■ **Workspace:** People are more productive when they have their own, predictable place to work, so try to carve out a specific location for your new hire. If you're hiring employees for your new restaurant or store, their workspace is pretty obvious. But if you work from a home office, finding a place for an employee to work may be one of your biggest issues. Do you want them working with you in the small spare bedroom you use for your office, or should they be at the dining room table?

■ **Storage:** Regardless of where your employee works, they need at least a small amount of space to store their own stuff: office supplies, files, coats, purses, and lunch. You might want to purchase some storage units or lockers (especially in a well-trafficked location like a restaurant).

■ **Equipment/furniture/supplies/services:** Where will your employee sit—literally? Do you have a chair and desk for them? This doesn't have to be expensive (many Silicon Valley startups use inexpensive folding tables as desks, and you can find a lot of used office furniture on websites such as Craigslist.org). What equipment, such as computers and phones, will they need? How about other supplies, uniforms, telecom or Internet services?

■ **Access:** When you worked alone, you didn't have to worry about privacy and security. Now you do. One thing to consider is how much and what kind of access you'll give your new employee to things such as your data, your facilities, and your personal items. Do you want to give your new employee a key to your office? Or will you wait a few months before entrusting them? Do you want your new administrative assistant to have access to your personal files or bank accounts, or do you want to set up password protection for such data? How will you keep private information—perhaps contracts or personal correspondence that you keep in your office—secure from others? Set some of these systems up before your new employee arrives.

■ **Working hours/days:** One of the first questions a prospect will ask you is "What are the working hours?" Figure out which days you want/need your new employee to work and which hours. Once again, if you work from home, do you want your employee to arrive after the kids are off to school and be gone before your spouse gets home?

Much of what you decide about all these logistics depends on your personal comfort level and preferences. Some people feel comfortable giving an employee a key to their own home; others don't want employees to even overhear their business phone conversations. There's no right or wrong—just what works for you.

Use the worksheet to jot down your thoughts about the logistics involved with hiring your employee.

worksheet: Logistics

Use this worksheet to identify your needs and preferences in regard to each of these logistical concerns relating to hiring a new employee.

	NEEDS/PREFERENCES
Workspace	
Furniture	
Equipment	
Supplies	
Services	
Storage	
Telecom	

	NEEDS/PREFERENCES
Work days	
Work hours	
Facilities access	
Data access	
Other:	
Other:	
Other:	
Other:	

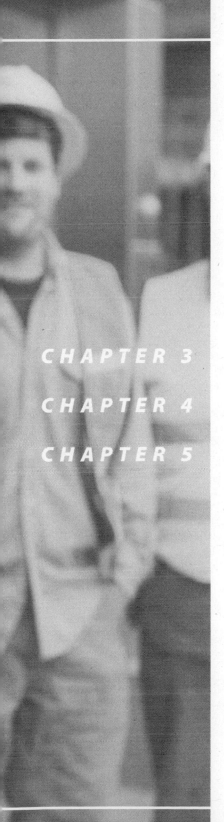

Section Two:
The Nitty Gritty— Employee Status, Labor Laws, Payroll and Taxes

CHAPTER 3 **Understanding Employee Status** *28*

CHAPTER 4 **Employment Law** *38*

CHAPTER 5 **Managing Payroll and Payroll Taxes** *46*

Understanding Employee Status

"Always treat your employees exactly as you want them to treat your best customers."
—STEPHEN R COVEY

Once you've decided to hire, you'll need at least a basic understanding of the many laws affecting how you, as an employer, treat the people who work for you. In the next few chapters, you'll learn about the basics of employment and labor law, payroll taxes, and ways to manage your payroll. But first you need to be aware of how the law deals with the day-to-day status and treatment of your employees.

Determining Your Worker's Status

You're ready to hire someone, and they're going to be your employee, right? Well, yes, but how do you classify that worker? You can hire them as an employee or independent contractor, for instance—but laws regulate your choice. As an employee, they might be covered by overtime and minimum wage laws or they might not. You might give them a contract or you might hire them in such a way that you can fire them whenever you need or want.

All of this matters, so you need to know the basics of what determines a worker's legal employment status. An employee's status in the eyes of the government helps determine how much control over a worker you have, how much you have to pay them and for what, what rights they have, how much tax you have to pay, and more.

When determining your employee's status—in the eyes of the law, the major categories are:

- Employee versus independent contractor
- Exempt versus non-exempt employee
- At-will versus contract employee
- Full-time versus part-time employee

Employee or Independent Contractor

Your business is growing—or you want it to grow—so you've got to get help. One of the first things you'll have to figure out is whether the person you hire will be an:

- Employee *or*

- Independent contractor

Few areas of tax law are murkier than—or can get a business in as much trouble as—the laws relating to classifying workers as employees versus independent contractors. The IRS and labor agencies aggressively pursue companies that intentionally—or unintentionally—classify someone as an independent contractor yet treat them as an employee. The IRS has gone after huge corporations as well as small businesses, and once they find a violation, they're likely to go back through many past years of your taxes. So be careful.

Many companies would prefer to classify workers as independent contractors rather than employees. Here's why:

- Employees are subject to payroll taxes and come under labor laws; independent contractors do not.

And some workers would rather be classified as independent contractors. Here's why:

- Independent contractors do not have payroll taxes deducted from each paycheck, and many of their business expenses are tax deductible.

While classifying workers as independent contractors may benefit you financially, even if both you and the worker agree to such classification, employment laws limit that choice. So it's important to understand the basic outline of what makes an employee an employee and under which circumstances you can classify them as an independent contractor.

Criteria for employee vs. independent contractor

In a nutshell, the question of who "controls" the worker determines that worker's status. The more control you have over the worker—such as when, where and how they work—the more likely the worker is your employee. The nature of the work they do for you does not alone determine their status.

The IRS and other government agencies prefer employers to classify their workers as employees. Why? Federal, state and city governments want to make certain that anyone doing the work of an employee gets treated as such. Employees are entitled to many legal protections, including rules regarding overtime and unemployment. And the government wants to protect as many workers as possible.

*HIRE*Learning

Form 1099-MISC for Independent Contractors

For each and every independent contractor you pay $600 or more in any calendar year, you must complete and file a Form 1099-MISC, which reports miscellaneous income to the IRS. It is due no later than January 31 of the year following the one in which the independent contractor worked for you. You must also give the independent contractor a copy of the 1099-MISC form by the same due date.

Also, because employers are legally responsible to withhold tax money from employees' salaries, government agencies can depend on receiving full, timely tax payments. Independent contractors, on the other hand, invoice employers and receive paychecks from which no deductions have been withheld. They manage their own tax payments and can be less reliable about submitting their taxes.

If you misclassify a worker, penalties will likely include fines and back taxes for:

- Employee and employer's share of Social Security and Medicare taxes

- Federal and State income taxes that should have been withheld

- Unemployment taxes

The IRS' unclear guidelines make classifying independent contractors even more difficult. However, the main issue the IRS uses to determine employee status is who "controls" the worker. The IRS once had a list of specific rules governing independent contractor status, but, responding to the legitimate needs of businesses for greater flexibility in hiring independent contractors, made the rules broader.

But this means there's more room for misunderstanding. The IRS looks at three areas:

1. **Behavioral.** Does the worker control how they do the work? The IRS looks at issues such as who determines the employee's work hours and location, who controls the order or sequence of the employee's work processes and who owns the tools or equipment the worker uses to get the job done.

2. **Type of relationship.** How permanent is the relationship? Is the work performed a critical and regular part of the business? Is there a written contract? Is the worker responsible for their own benefits?

3. **Financial.** Does the worker have a significant investment—i.e., do they own their own tools? Do they make their services available to other and/or work for other businesses?

Because the rules are somewhat fuzzy, the IRS does provide some protections for businesses that make mistakes in treating employees as independent contractors—as long as those mistakes were made in good faith. They'll investigate whether a business relied on the advice of an attorney or accountant, followed industry practice, and acted consistently.

Here's More from the IRS:

Businesses must weigh all these factors when determining whether a worker is an employee or independent contractor. Some factors may indicate that the worker is an employee, while other factors indicate that the worker is an independent contractor. There is no "magic" or set number of factors that "makes" the worker an employee or an independent contractor, and no one factor stands alone in making this determination. Also, factors which are relevant in one situation may not be relevant in another. The keys are to look at the entire relationship, consider the degree or extent of the right to direct and control, and finally, to document each of the factors used in coming up with the determination.

—U.S. Internal Revenue Service

But—and this is important—there's absolutely *no protection* for a company that doesn't file the necessary tax forms for independent contractors. Each year, you must file 1099-MISC forms which report payment to independent contractors over a certain dollar figure. If you fail to file 1099's and the IRS later challenges you on the classification of your independent contractors, you're in very hot water.

Review the "Right Classification" Table for the criteria the IRS uses to evaluate control of a worker and therefore how they are classified. Remember, you run into danger by misclassifying an employee as an independent contractor, and never the other way 'round. The IRS won't tell you that you should have classified an employee as an independent contractor.

If you have doubts about how to classify a new worker, request an employee status determination from the IRS. To do so, both you and your employee will file IRS Form SS-8, *Determination of Worker Status for Purposes of Federal Employment Taxes and Income Tax Withholding*, available online at www.irs.gov. Until you hear back from the IRS, deduct and submit taxes as you would for an employee. If the IRS decides your employee is a contractor, you can apply for a refund of those taxes. If the IRS decides your employee is in fact an employee, you have saved yourself time, money and a headache.

If you plan on using independent contractors in addition to employees, ask your attorney about how to stay well within the law, and check with your accountant about filing all necessary tax forms.

Employee vs. Independent Contractor: The Right Classification

EMPLOYEES...	INDEPENDENT CONTRACTORS...
Do not run their own business	Are independent business people, especially if they are incorporated
Work in your office and use equipment you provide	Choose their work location and provide their own equipment, tools and materials
Work hours specified by you	Set their own hours
Work per your instructions and may receive training from you	Decide how to perform their services, in what order, and usually receive no training
Are paid for their labor regardless of business performance	Can earn a profit or suffer a loss depending on the quality an quantity of services they provide
Work for you on a continuing basis	Manage multiple clients or customers and work for you on an as-needed project basis
Receive employee benefits	Are responsible for their own benefits
Are usually paid by unit of time	Are usually paid a flat rate or by project
Can quit or be fired at any time	Can be terminated or leave according the terms of their agreement with you

When Temporary Employees Make Sense

If you need extra help for a busy time or for special projects, consider a temporary employee. A worker sent to you by an agency is employed by that agency, and therefore payroll, taxes and insurance are covered by the agency. Expect to pay more than if you hired the workers directly. You're paying for convenience.

When your peak period slows back to normal, you simply end the employee lease—without damaging morale as you would laying off a permanent employee. Some agencies specialize in fields such as office workers, accountants, graphic designers or tech workers. These trained temporary employees can often start immediately, without the learning curve that can come with a new employee.

What's right for you? Employees or independent contractors

Let's say you run a restaurant. You must have waiters and cooks who come in on certain days, at certain times, and perform certain tasks (such as waiting on tables). These workers are employees; there's almost no way that waiters and cooks could be legally classified as independent contractors.

But in other cases, you can make the decision whether to hire an employee or engage an independent contractor instead.

For instance, let's also say you need a marketing manager for your restaurant. You want your marketing manager to run your website, send out press releases, and call prospects to hold events at your restaurant. Should you hire a part-time marketing specialist or should you engage a marketing consultant who'll be an independent contractor?

If you hired an employee, you could have your marketing director come in to the restaurant's office at times set by you and work on your computer. You'd be certain that they were actually doing the work they were hired to do. If you didn't like the way they were doing something, you could correct them and show them how you'd like it done. Under the law, that marketing director must be classified as an employee. You'd have the extra expenses of payroll taxes and workspace and equipment. But your marketing director would be part of your team; you'd know whether or not she was doing her job; you could call on her for other tasks.

Instead, if you hired a marketing consultant to perform those tasks, and that consultant worked from her own home, at times she chose, using her own computer—and especially if she had other clients—she would certainly be considered an independent contractor. You wouldn't have to pay her payroll taxes or provide any company benefits. She'd use her own equipment, and that would save you money too. On the other hand, her hourly fee might be higher—perhaps much higher—than if she were your employee. And—importantly—would you be as confident that she was making as many calls or sending out as many press releases as if she were working under your direction? You have more control over employees than you do independent contractors.

Most businesses use independent contractors at some point—especially to do specific projects or tasks. It's likely you'll use an independent contractor to help you with your legal, accounting, technology, or marketing needs. In fact, it's possible to build quite a "virtual" company using many independent contractors—even legally. But some tasks are not appropriate—or legal—for independent contractors.

It's likely that independent contractors will have less of a long-term (as well as day-to-day) commitment to you. They may choose to stop working for you. While the money-saving upside seems compelling, not all workers qualify as independent contractors *and* it's not always the best choice for you.

Advantages of having employees:

1. You have control. Employees work for you; you can tell them when and where you want them to work and exactly how you want them to get the job done. You can provide on-the-job training so they do the work exactly how you want.

2. You—or a member of your staff—can see and supervise employees. That way, you are certain that they are performing the work in the time you are paying them for. You can see how productive each employee is.

3. Employees often feel a deep sense of attachment to their jobs and employers, feeling part of a team. They are more likely to have a sense of commitment to your company.

4. Employees are likely to want to stay long term, adding consistency and legacy knowledge to your team.

5. If an employee creates anything that might be considered intellectual property—whether it's your company logo, a design, software, website content, or the like—while working on the job, you automatically own the rights to that work.

6. Employees are often far cheaper on an hourly basis.

Advantages of using independent contractors:

1. None of the payroll taxes and employee-related laws apply to independent contractors, so you won't pay Social Security and Medicare taxes or workers compensation and unemployment insurance, and you don't have to worry about overtime pay or complying with other labor laws. Paperwork is easier, too.

2. You do not provide benefits—such as health care—to independent contractors. Once again, this can save you a considerable amount of money.

3. Independent contractors tend to bring special skills and experience to the job you've hired them for. They generally don't need training.

4. Independent contractors provide their own supplies and workspace, lowering your overhead.

5. Most independent contractors are motivated to do a good job, since they want to keep you as a client and get referrals from you. Since you typically hire them on a project basis, you don't have to worry about finding continuous work for them or laying them off if business is slow.

Independent Contractor Agreements

When working with an independent contractor, clarify your project's scope, goals and expectations by drawing up an Independent Contractor Agreement. You can use this agreement to demonstrate the intended contractor relationship to the IRS, if needed. Include information such as the services to be rendered, the manner of billing, how much and when you will pay your contractor, location of services, the contractor's tax identification number, and any other information that will help clarify your expectations and your contractor's role. If they are creating anything for you—such as designs, software, logos—make sure you have a "work-for-hire" clause so that you retain ownership of their work product. An online search of independent contractor agreements will turn up many samples upon which you can build yours.

Exempt vs. Non-Exempt Employees

Once you've classified a worker as an *employee*, the next most important thing you have to figure out is whether—in the eyes of the law—they are *exempt* or *non-exempt* from the Fair Labor and Standards Act (FLSA).

The FLSA of 1938 established a national minimum wage, guaranteed time and a half overtime pay for certain jobs, set standards for the employment of minors and prohibited oppressive child labor, and established guidelines for employer recordkeeping. These employment standards apply to employees in the private sector and in Federal, State and local governments.

■ **Non-Exempt:** Employees who are covered by the Fair Labor and Standards Act and, by extension, by most state and city labor laws. You must pay them at least the federal (and state) minimum wage, and they must receive overtime pay of 1.5 their regular rate of pay when they work more than 40 hours in a week.

More from the Department of Labor

Section 13(a)(1) of the FLSA provides an exemption from both *minimum wage* and *overtime pay* for employees employed as bona fide executive, administrative, professional and outside sales employees. Section 13(a)(1) and Section 13(a)(17) also exempt certain computer employees. To qualify for exemption, employees generally must meet certain tests regarding their job duties and be paid on a salary basis at not less than $455 per week. Job titles do not determine exempt status. In order for an exemption to apply, an employee's specific job duties and salary must meet all the requirements of the Department's regulations.

—U.S. Department of Labor

■ **Exempt:** Employees who are NOT covered by FLSA laws. They do not have to be paid overtime or minimum wage, however to be exempt, they must meet criteria relating to their job responsibilities and minimum pay level.

Federal laws are often augmented with state or local labor laws that mandate additional worker protections, such as paid lunch breaks or other breaks, for non-exempt workers.

Once again, determining exactly who can be considered exempt can sometimes be murky. But here's what the government tries to accomplish—protect wage earners, especially those who perform routine work for the lowest wages, often on an hourly basis. They want to make certain these workers are not mis-used—overworked without additional pay, paid below minimum wage, and so on.

On the other hand, the government wants to leave businesses reasonable flexibility with other types of employees. For example, it would be downright silly to require a major corporation to give an executive, earning hundreds of thousands of dollars a year, overtime pay just for working more than 40 hours a week.

Once again, it can sometimes be challenging to determine whether someone is exempt or non-exempt. The main criteria are:

■ **Salary level:** Exempt employees must earn a minimum of $455 per week; employees earning less than that are almost certainly non-exempt. Highly paid salaried workers (over $100,000) are virtually always exempt.

■ **Salaried versus hourly pay basis:** Many employers wrongly believe that if they pay a worker a salary, the worker is automatically exempt. Wrong! The worker must still meet the minimum pay amounts.

■ **Professions/jobs:** Certain types of jobs are exempt, such as professional, administrative, outside sales, and technical computer employees who are paid at least $27.63 per hour. Certain types of jobs are non-exempt, such as manual workers, and blue collar workers (such as construction, production workers, etc), no matter how much they are paid.

- **Duties/Responsibilities:** Professional and administrative personnel must also meet criteria relating to the types of duties they perform. These criteria can include responsibilities for the management of the business, supervision or training of others, exercise of independent judgment and the like.

A salesperson working in a department store for $9 an hour is not going to be exempt. A salesperson earning a salary of $500 a week also won't be exempt even though she is paid on a salaried basis and earns more than the minimum amount required. An administrative assistant who is paid $600 a week but does routine clerical duties will be non-exempt. An administrative assistant paid $600 a week who runs the office, hires, trains, and supervises the clerical staff, and decides on business insurance *may* be exempt.

Whether someone qualifies for exempt or non-exempt status is extremely important as it relates to issues such as overtime pay and many state labor laws. So do take a bit of time to familiarize yourself with the basic concept.

At Will vs. Contract Employees

As a new employer, you'll want to become familiar with the concept of "at will" employment. Most businesses in the US hire employees on at "at will basis." Most likely, you'll hire your employees on an "at will" basis, rather than with an individual or union contract. If you draw up a contract with an employee—perhaps to spell out job duties and payments—be sure to specify that they're still hired on an "at will" basis.

Under employment "at will" laws, you can terminate someone with or without reason—at any time. That's a great ability to have. Of course, your employee can also quit at any time for no reason. But hiring employees on at "at will" employment status gives you the most control over when you can fire someone or lay them off and the most flexibility with your staffing if you run into financial difficulties.

Although the law assumes that employment is "at will," it's a good practice to draw up a job offer letter which has your new employee acknowledge the fact that they're hired "at will" in writing. If you need assistance, consult a lawyer knowledgeable about employment law. (See the sample job offer letter in Chapter 11—Finding and Hiring the Right Employee.)

What can get you in trouble with "at will" employment status

While hiring employees "at will," gives you great latitude in firing or layoffs, you can still get into trouble and there are restrictions on why you can fire someone. You could end up with a "wrongful termination" lawsuit from a fired employee—even one hired on at "at will" basis. It doesn't take much to avoid these potential problems.

There are a few exceptions to the "at will" status, but the ones you want to pay most attention to—as a new employer are these:

- **Breach of implied contract.** Be careful not to make direct or implied promises you can't keep, especially regarding job security. Never state verbally or in a document things such as "Employees won't be fired except for just cause" or "No matter what happens, you can count on a job for the next year." Most states have laws that treat implied contracts as an exception to "at will" status.

- **Discrimination.** Make certain you don't violate any anti-discrimination laws when you fire or lay off employees. Covered classes—when it comes to unlawful discrimination—include age, race, sex, national origin, religion, disability. So even if you can fire someone "at will," make sure you can justify why you are firing someone or laying off one employee and not another, especially if they're in a covered class.

- **Breach of good faith and fair dealings.** Some states limit the "at will" status if a firing is done for any reason other than just cause.

- **Violation of public policy.** You can not fire someone "at will" if doing so undermines or violates public policy or the public good. For instance, you can not fire someone for taking advantage of their legal rights—such as filing a workmen's compensation claim or taking advantage of the Family and Medical Leave Act.

- **Breach of contract.** If you sign a contract with an employee, then you must follow the terms of the contract. For instance, if you state that an employee will be hired for a minimum of two years, the contract supersedes "at will" status, unless there are other contract provisions that allow you to fire that employee.

Because the "at will" status gives you as an employer so much flexibility, make certain you don't undermine that status. Have new employees sign a document making clear they understand they are hired "at will," and do not do anything to imply that they have unlimited job security.

Contract and Union Employees

When you hire an employee under a contract, the contractual terms generally trump the "at will" status. Make certain, even if you have a contract with a new employee, that you still specify that their employment is "at will" and that you retain the right to terminate them at any time without cause.

When might you give someone a contract? Let's say you are starting a new video gaming company, and your company's growth depends on your ability to entice an exceptionally-talented game designer/programmer to come work for you. That job candidate might insist on a contract before leaving their job and taking a chance on you. In which case, you'll have to negotiate a contract with them. If so, get the help of an experienced labor attorney, because you want to make sure you still have an out if you experience financial difficulties and that you,

personally, will not be responsible for their salary or other benefits if the company fails.

A bigger issue for your business is the likelihood of creating an *implied contract* by making statements that could be seen as contractual in a lawsuit. For instance, if you have a personnel manual that says employees will only be fired for a just cause, that could be viewed as a contract. If you tell someone they will receive annual raises, that could be viewed as a contract. So be careful about any promises you make to employees that could undermine the "at will" status.

As for union contracts, as a new employer or small business, it's highly unlikely you'll face issues with union contracts, but those, too, could trump the "at will" status. However, your employees won't be union members, and if you treat your employees well and pay them fairly, you won't be the target of any union organizing attempts.

Full-Time or Part-Time Employees?

Many new employers think it matters a great deal whether they classify workers as full-time or part-time employees. And it does—from your business point-of-view. It certainly costs you more total dollars when you hire someone full-time—especially if you don't need a worker full-time. You may also decide that only workers who work a certain minimum number of hours per week, let's say 30 or 35 hours, are entitled to employee benefits, such as health insurance.

But from the government's point-of-view, full-time employees and part-time employees are treated the same way. In fact, permanent employees and those hired for only short periods (such as the holiday season) are treated the same. For tax purposes—such as Social Security, Medicare, and unemployment—full-time and part-time are treated the same. For protections under the federal or state labor laws, they're the same.

So feel free to hire employees on either a full-time or part-time basis. But it doesn't change your responsibilities to them under the law.

Hanna Design Limited
Creative, Low-Budget Staffing Pays Off

When Cindy Hanna started her graphic design business in 1982, Hanna Design Limited, she was working in the smallest space available in her suburban Denver home: the laundry room. Good thing her only employee was a cat named Snowflake. Working during her infant son's naps and at night, Hanna built a small and loyal client roster. Since then, the business has grown in many ways, not the least of which is in the number of employees and amount of office space.

Even when she was the lone employee, Hanna knew she couldn't do it all and, to her credit, knew precisely what she didn't have the expertise to do. "I didn't trust myself to do the books," she admits. She asked around and found an outsourced bookkeeper that would come to her home office each month, collect the receipts and invoices, and magically return with prepared financial statements.

A classically trained, pencil-in-hand designer, Hanna struggled with the transition to computer-based design work. Her next hire, a Mac-savvy part-time designer, not only brought the company into the computer age but allowed Hanna to focus more on business development and concept-level design work.

In the late 1980s and early '90s, Hanna saw a surge of work on the horizon and knew she needed to staff-up, but couldn't take on the risk of a large team of full-time employees.

Instead, she created a staffing model that lowered her risk, attracted top design talent, and allowed the business to flourish. "After talking with my lawyer and accountant, I devised a way in which I would bring on selected freelance designers, offer them reduced rent on space in our offices, and have them work at an hourly rate on our clients' work," she explains. The freelance designers had access to workstations complete with computers, printers, network connections, etc.—as well as conference room access to work on their own clients' projects. Using this innovative approach, Hanna assembled a team of designers capable of wowing clients without the burden of full-time wages and benefits. Meanwhile, the designers had a steady stream of regular work, discounted rent on terrific office space and the autonomy freelancers seek. It's an approach she still uses today.

As her company approaches its 30th year, Hanna credits its growth on the team she's built and the work they continue to produce for clients. Today, Hanna Design consists of full- and part-time employees, outsourced services (books and payroll), and freelancers who work under the tried-and-true model that made the company successful. "That was the best decision I made in growing the business," Hanna says.

Employment and Labor Law—The Basics

> *"What the world really needs is more love and less paperwork."*
> —PEARL BAILEY

Over the years, labor laws have been enacted—some by the Federal government, most by individual states, covering many aspects of what you can and can not do as an employer. These laws have been designed to make sure that workers are treated fairly, but you may be surprised at the broad range of areas the laws cover, including:

- What questions you are not allowed to ask in an interview
- How many hours an employee can work before you must pay them overtime and how much that overtime must be
- The need to give employees lunch breaks and other breaks and how long those must be
- Which workers you must treat as employees and which ones you can treat as independent contractors

Because of the sheer number of laws, you won't be able to learn them all—you'd need to become a labor attorney. Thank goodness, that's not necessary.

But, as an employer, it's a good idea to familiarize yourself with the most basic federal and state labor laws to help you both develop the best practices and stay out of trouble.

Keep in mind that you must obey labor laws mandated both by the federal government and also by your own state, and in a few cases, perhaps by your city. Each state has enacted its own set of regulations governing employment and these are typically more broad-reaching than federal law. For instance, federal law does not require you to give employees lunch breaks, but about half of the US states do. And each of those state laws varies.

This chapter outlines what you absolutely must know as an employer—the most critical labor laws—and shows you where you can get the most up-to-date information. Keep in mind a basic premise: the best way to stay out of trouble is to always treat your employees fairly and decently.

Key Labor Laws

Don't let the fact that there are so many laws governing employment scare you—just become familiar with the basics, and you'll almost certainly stay out of trouble. Most entrepreneurs quickly find themselves knowledgeable enough about these regulations to know when they might be getting into an area covered by the law, at which point they realize they better ask a lawyer or seek more guidance.

Below is a guide to the major areas of employment law that you'll need to know about and which basic laws apply on a federal level and may apply on a state level (and in some very rare cases, on a city level).

Minimum wage

Federal law: As of 2010, the federal minimum wage of $7.25 per hour applies to all *non-exempt* workers (see the previous chapter—basically all non-professional, non-managerial workers) with a few exceptions (student learners, some disabled workers or full-time students, youth under 20 years of age for the first 90 days on the job). If you pay workers on a piece-work basis, the amount must still equal at least the minimum wage per hour. If your employees earn tips, *federal* law allows you to include tips when determining minimum wage, although you still must pay them a minimum of $2.13 per hour, even with tip credit.

State law: Many states have their own minimum wage laws. If your state or city sets minimum wage higher than the federal minimum wage, you must pay the employee the higher of the two. A few states have a lower minimum wage, but the lower minimum wage only applies if the business is not covered by FLSA—an unlikely occurrence for most employers. If your state has a lower minimum wage, definitely check with an attorney before paying any employee below federal minimum wage levels. Also, a number of states require tipped employees to get higher minimum wages than the federal level.

What's Legal vs. What's Right

Dealing with the seemingly endless labyrinth of laws regulating the hiring of employees, you may begin to feel overwhelmed. There are laws regarding workplace safety, discrimination, overtime, dealing with individuals with disabilities, and more. Obviously, you must comply with these legal mandates. But there's a difference between doing just the minimum required by law and doing the right thing. You want to be fair, establish an atmosphere of respect and trust, and treat people decently without being mean or abusive. Don't just do the minimum. Do what any ethical and caring individual would do for fellow human beings.

Overtime, working hours, meal and other breaks

Federal law: Non-exempt workers covered by FLSA must receive one and one-half times their regular rate of pay after 40 hours of work in any one week. However, this overtime law does not cover exempt workers—managerial, professional, and some computer workers. Federal law does not mandate lunch or other meal breaks—if you give them (and why wouldn't you for full-time workers?), they do not have to be paid. But if an employee eats lunch at their desk and does work (such as answering the phone), they must be paid. Also, short breaks—to use the bathroom or get a cup of coffee, for instance—are considered part of the work day and must be paid. Other time that is considered paid work time includes any mandatory training, on-call or waiting time at the workplace and time traveling as part of the job (not including commuting to/from work).

State law: Many states have more rigorous rules regarding work hours and break time than the federal government does. For example, many states require lunch breaks or paid rest breaks. Make sure you understand the law for your state to avoid problems.

Time off, required leaves

Federal law: The Family and Medical Leave Act (FMLA) ensures that workers will not be fired if they have to take time off because of the birth or adoption of a child or because of their own or a family member's "serious health condition." The law requires employers to provide up to 12 weeks *unpaid* leave, continue health care coverage during that time (if that benefit is provided), and protect their job upon their return. At the federal level, FMLA only applies to businesses with at least 50 employees. Other federal laws protect workers called up for military service. Employers must preserve these workers' jobs or provide them with a similar job upon their return. There are no federal requirements for paid holidays, vacation, sick leave, or bereavement leave.

State law: This is an area in which many states mandate more generous benefits for employees. Some states have more lenient family and medical leave regulations. Many states require paid time off for jury duty. Some states are considering the adoption of paid sick leave rules.

Equal opportunity/discrimination

Federal law: Federal law is designed to ensure, as much as possible, that workplaces are free of discrimination and of any kind of discriminatory atmosphere. To that end, the law prohibits *any form* of employment discrimination on the basis of:

■ Race

■ Age

■ Sex

■ Religion

■ Color

■ National origin

■ Disability

The rules are very sweeping. You're not permitted to discriminate: when hiring, advertising, or recruiting for a job; in terms of pay, benefits or any form of compensation; in promotions or layoffs; in the use of facilities or any other form of discrimination. You also can not discriminate against someone because they are married to, or associated with, an individual of a particular race, religion, national origin, or disability. You can't harass someone or create a hostile work environment. You can't discriminate against someone because they have an accent or because they have characteristics common to certain ethnic or national groups. You can't discriminate on the basis of pregnancy. That means that in a job interview, you can't ask a question about whether a candidate intends to start a family.

You also are required to make "reasonable accommodation" for employees' religious practices. So if an employee can not work on a religious holiday, and you can reasonably adjust their schedule, you must do so.

Although the federal laws only apply to businesses with at least 15 employees (20 in the case of age), you should follow these practices no matter how small your business is.

State law: States also have their own enforcement agencies and mechanisms to implement these laws.

Equal pay for equal work

Federal law: The Equal Pay Act (EPA) requires all businesses to provide equal pay (and other compensation) for equal work to both men and women. It doesn't matter if the jobs have different titles: if the work is substantially the same, and requires the same skills, you must pay the same wages. In other words, if you hire a male to fill the job of office coordinator and he has the same responsibilities, performs essentially the same work, and has the same level of experience as a female administrative assistant, you must pay them the same wages. Exceptions are allowed for genuine, objective differences in seniority, merit, and incentives that both men and women have equal access to.

State law: States also have their own enforcement agencies and mechanisms to implement these laws.

Hiring the disabled

Federal Law: The Americans with Disabilities Act (ADA) prohibits employment discrimination for any business with 15 or more employees. The term "disability" is broadly defined—it covers anyone with any kind of physical or mental disease or disability. You may not refuse to hire someone based only on their disability nor may you refuse to promote them, pay them less, or harass them (or allow other employees to harass them). However, the person must meet normal job requirements (such as previous experience or education) and be able to perform the job functions. You may be required to make "reasonable accommodation" to enable disabled employees to do their job. Note: you are not allowed to ask a job candidate any questions about their medical condition, history or disability or require them to undergo a medical examination until after you have made a job offer. You can, however, ask them whether they can satisfy the job requirements. If you hire disabled workers, you may be eligible for some federal tax incentives, especially if you must spend money for reasonable accommodation.

State law: Some states have other resources to assist workers and job-seekers with disabilities.

Child labor laws

Federal law: In almost all cases, the minimum age for non-farm employment is 16, but no one under 18 can work in hazardous conditions. Teenagers who are 14 or 15 may work in some occupations, outside of school hours only, and the work hours are limited—both in duration and time of day. (No more than 3 hours in a school day—18 hours total in a school week; 8 hours on a non-school day—40 hours total in a non-school week; not before 7 am or after 7 pm/9 pm summer.) There are exceptions for farm workers, certain occupations (such as theatrical performance and newspaper delivery) and working for parents. There are specific record keeping requirements when you employ those under 19 years of age. A worker over 18 years of age is not covered by child labor laws.

State law: Many states have even more stringent laws protecting children and youth. In all cases, whichever law provides the greatest protection is the one you must follow.

HIRELearning

Fair Labor and Standards Act

The main federal law governing labor laws is the Fair Labor Standards Act (FLSA), first enacted in 1938, and revised and broadened regularly. There are seven main aspects to the FLSA that you need to know about and comply with: which employees are covered by the FLSA; minimum wage; overtime pay; child labor; equal pay for equal work; posting requirements; record keeping requirements.

Employees who are not covered by FLSA are considered exempt and are generally professional, managerial and technical workers. Some employers may also not be covered for certain regulation— for instance, small businesses that gross less than $500,000 a year and are not, in any way, engaged in interstate commerce. However, "interstate commerce" is defined very broadly—even using telephones and the mail to conduct business can qualify—so it's almost certain you'll be covered by FLSA. Any questions? Check the FLSA Advisor act www.dol.gov.

Labor Laws—What's Legal and What's Not

SCENARIO	LEGAL?	WHY OR WHY NOT?
You're a general contractor. For a flat fee of $100, you hire a painter to paint an office. He completes the job in 20 hours.	Illegal	If you compensate an employee on a piece-work basis, the hourly wage must add up to at least the minimum wage in your state. Depending on your state, you must pay this painter at least $145 for the work (federal minimum wage of $7.25 an hour x 20 hours).
You prepare to open your new retail clothing store. You hire three sales clerks and train them for two days before your grand opening. When the store opens, you will pay them $9/hour. For training, you pay them the minimum wage.	Legal	You must compensate employees for time they spend in training. You can pay them the minimum wage. Be sure to inform them of their hourly rate for training sessions.
You operate a restaurant in Arizona and pay your new server $4.25 an hour. In a 40 hour work week, he earns another $120 in tips, or $3 an hour.	Legal	An employer in Arizona may pay a tipped employee up to $3 below the minimum wage as long as that employee earns enough in weekly tips to add up to the minimum wage in Arizona ($7.25/hour in 2010).
Your restaurant in Arizona does so well that you open your doors in California. You pay a new server $5 an hour. In a forty hour work week, she earns $200 a week in tips, an extra $5 an hour.	Illegal	In California, employers must pay their tipped employees at least the minimum wage ($8.00/hour in 2010), regardless of how much extra those employees earn in tips.
You hire an inside salesperson to work in your shoe store full time. You pay him a wage of $6 an hour plus a 5% commission on sales. During his first week, he earns $25 in commission, plus wages of $240.	Illegal	Your inside salesperson's wages must add up to at least the minimum wage. In this case, the salesperson earned a gross of $265 for the week, or $6.63 an hour, which is below the national minimum wage.
Just before the summer rush, you hire an experienced inside salesperson to work in your marina full time. You pay her straight commission. During her first week, she earns $1200 in commission.	Legal	Although you do not pay any direct wages to your inside salesperson, she earns a wage well above the minimum.
You have a big rush order for your widgets. Your shipping clerk works late one night, bringing her total hours to 50 for the week. She earns her regular wage of $8/hour for a total of $360 for the week.	Illegal	You must pay your employee overtime for the hours which exceed forty hours for the week. Your shipping clerk must be paid $12/hour for the additional ten hours, bringing her gross pay to $440 for the week.
Your salaried director of logistics also works 50 hours during the week of the rush order. You don't pay him overtime.	Legal	You do not have to pay exempt employees overtime wages. (See Chapter 3 on Understanding Employee Status.)
You hire a 15 year old high school student to bus tables in the summer at your beach front restaurant. During the week of a busy water-front festival, he works overtime for 12 hours and you pay him overtime for those extra 12 hours.	Illegal	Children aged 14 and 15 can not work over 40 hours a week, even during non-school weeks. Teens and youths aged 16 or older, however, can work overtime.

SCENARIO	LEGAL?	WHY OR WHY NOT?
When the summer season ends, you cut back your busboy's hours. He works three hours on both Thursdays and Fridays, from four to seven in the evening. He also works for eight hours every Saturday.	Legal	Teens under the age of 16 can work up to three hours a day on a school day, eight hours a day on a non-school day, and 18 hours a week in a school week. Your busboy's hours fall within these regulations.
You own a busy photography studio. You hire a student intern over the summer to work for free in exchange for experience in the field.	Illegal	Student interns can work for free only if they receive college credit in exchange for their work. Contact your intern's college to find out their requirements for setting up an internship program.
You and your husband own a bakery. Your 13 year old helps you mix, knead and bake bread on Saturday mornings.	Legal	Children 13 and younger can work for their parents who own and operate businesses.
You hire a full-time nanny to take care of your kids while you start up your graphic design business. You pay the nanny cash and you don't pay payroll taxes or file anything with the IRS.	Illegal	Illegal. You must pay payroll taxes on domestic workers. (See Chapter 5 on Managing Payroll and Payroll Taxes.)
You offer health insurance benefits to your employees. Because your employees are covered by health insurance, you think you don't have to register for workers' compensation.	Illegal	Workers' compensation is legally required. Health insurance coverage does not replace it.
You hire a new office administrator. He shows you his U.S. Passport to prove his American citizenship. You do not take further action.	Illegal	All of your employees, regardless of citizenship, must fill out a Form I-9, the Employment Eligibility Verification Form, within three days of their first day of employment.

For More Info

Though the laws are many and some of them complex, the government has a number of websites for more information. Start with www.Business.gov—the federal government's entry-point website for business. Also check the U.S. Department of Labor's Web site (www.dol.gov). Use the search term "state labor offices" to find links to your state's site. If you have any questions about employment laws, contact your state's labor department. And it's always a very good idea to seek advice from an attorney familiar with labor laws in your state.

Eligibility to work

Federal law: You can only hire American citizens or non-citizens who have the right to work in the US. In other words, you can not hire undocumented workers who are not legally entitled to work in the United States. By Federal law, you are responsible for verifying an employee's right to work in the US, and you must complete an "Employment Eligibility/ Verification Form"—called an "I9"—within three days after you hire someone. You must keep this form on record for three years after hire or one year after termination (whichever is later). You do not file this form with the government.

State law: Federal law governs eligibility to work in the US. A few states have enacted laws requiring certain employers (particularly those contracting with the state) to verify the eligibility status of all their employees using the federal government's "E-Verify" system.

Workplace safety and health

Federal law: The Occupational Safety and Health Act (OSHA) is designed to protect all workers from unsafe or unhealthy conditions on the job. OSHA has a wide range of regulations; the rules vary to some degree by industry. But OSHA regulations cover things such as exposure to chemicals, working with machinery, noise levels, fire safety, evacuation routes, confined spaces, and much, much more. You'll need assistance to make certain you're complying with OSHA rules, especially if your business involves working with construction, manufacturing, production, service, health care, machinery, or any other business that could potentially pose hazards to workers. OSHA provides a free consultation service.

State law: All states and most counties and large cities have a range of permits, regulations, certification requirements and other rules relating to conducting business under safe and healthy conditions for many, many types of businesses, protecting both workers and the public. If you're opening a restaurant, a hair salon, a dry cleaners, a manufacturing plant, a construction company, or a host of other types of businesses, you'll find that you come under state laws pertaining to your working conditions.

HIRELearning

E-Verify

To enable employers to check employees' eligibility to work in the US, the federal government created the "E-Verify" system, run by the Department of Homeland Security (DHS) in partnership with the Social Security Administration (SSA). This free online program allows participating employers to electronically check whether an employee is either a citizen or other documented worker and to check Social Security numbers.

Posters and record keeping

Federal law: To ensure that you comply with all applicable employment laws, the federal government requires you to maintain adequate records relating to every employee. These records document items such as employment history, pay and benefits, time used for family and medical leave, eligibility for employment, and the like. Rules vary for how long you must keep these records, but as a good rule of thumb, keep your records for at least three to four years after a worker leaves your employ. The federal government also requires you to post notices of the full range of employees' rights in a prominent place where employees can see them. The easiest way to accomplish this is to purchase a poster from one of the many private companies that sell them. You can get one that lists both federal and your state's laws generally for around $25. Just type "employment law poster" into a search engine.

State law: Like the federal government, most states require you to keep employment records and to post notices of employee's rights.

worksheet: Employment Laws as They Apply to Me

Complete this worksheet to list which employment laws apply to your business. Some states have stricter laws than the Federal government, and you usually must follow the law that gives employees the greatest protection. Find state laws on the Department of Labor's website www.dol.gov. Type in the search term "state labor offices."

	FEDERAL LAW	MY STATE'S LAW	WHAT I NEED TO DO
Minimum wage			
Overtime			
Working hours			
Meals			
Breaks			
Unpaid leave			
Hiring the disabled			
Child labor laws			
Eligibility to work			
Record keeping			
Workplace posters			

chapter

5

Managing Payroll and Payroll Taxes

> *The income tax has made more liars out of the American people than golf has.*
> —WILL ROGERS

As you plan for your first employees, you also have to figure out how you'll actually pay them. Paying your employees involves more than simply mailing out checks or depositing funds directly into your workers' checking accounts. You have to figure out payroll taxes, deductions, and benefits each and every pay period. And you have to do it right.

Payroll Basics

The government—federal, state, and sometimes local—takes all this very seriously, and you can get in expensive trouble if you mess up. So it's not just you and your workers you have to consider when you're choosing how to handle payroll.

First, the government wants to ensure that you pay your employees for the work they've done and the time they've put in—and they want you to pay on time. In fact, the law stipulates that you meet these obligations.

Next, the government wants to make certain you—and your employees—pay all necessary taxes on time and accurately. Additionally, the government uses you—as the employer—to help collect income taxes from your employees.

That's why it's absolutely critical that you develop a systematic method—or use a payroll service—to take care of paying your employees and collecting and paying all payroll and withholding taxes. Whether you do all the paperwork yourself, use an accountant, or use a payroll service, taking care of payroll is one of your most critical—and legally necessary—business tasks.

learn the lingo: Payroll Taxes and Managing Payroll

Compensation	All cash and non-cash payment given to an employee for services performed.
Deductions	The extra amounts subtracted from an employee's gross pay to reach net pay. Deductions can be made for benefits, such as health care, as well as retirement contributions.
Direct deposit	The electronic transfer of an employee's net pay directly into a bank account designated by the employee.
FEIN (Federal Employer Identification Number)	A number used by the IRS to identify a specific business, much as a Social Security number identifies an individual. Employers must have an FEIN. There are always nine digits in the following format: 00-0000000.
FICA (Federal Insurance Contributions Act)	This tax includes both Social Security and Medicare taxes. Both the employer and employee pay FICA taxes. The employer withholds the employee's portion from pay and sends it to the government.
FIT (Federal Income Tax)	A tax the federal government collects from employees based on personal or business income.
FUTA (Federal Unemployment Tax Act)	FUTA funds unemployment compensation programs to assist workers when terminated or laid off. The employer pays this federal tax, not the employee.
Garnishment	Attached wages required by court order for the payment of an employee's debts and obligations, such as child support.
Gross wages	Total earned income before any payroll deductions.
Independent contractor	Self-employed workers who provide services to a business on a non-employee basis. An employer does not pay employment taxes for or provide benefits to these types of workers. These workers must meet a strict IRS standard of independence to be legally classified as a "contractor".
Net pay	Also called "take-home pay." What's left after all payroll withholding and deductions.
Pay period	The standard time frame a paycheck covers, such as two weeks or half a month.
Wages	Compensation paid to employees based on work performed. Often usually based on an hourly or monthly rate.
Withholding	Taxes the employer deducts from the employee's pay and submits to the government. The amount withheld is based on wages and the number of allowances claimed by each employee on the W-4 form.

Anatomy of a Paycheck

There's no regulated or required format for paychecks and paystubs, but you'll find the same basic information on most paychecks:

Employee information

Employee's pay rate and the total number of hours worked during the pay period, if applicable.

Net amount paid after all withholding and deductions

Employer information

Total gross payment being made

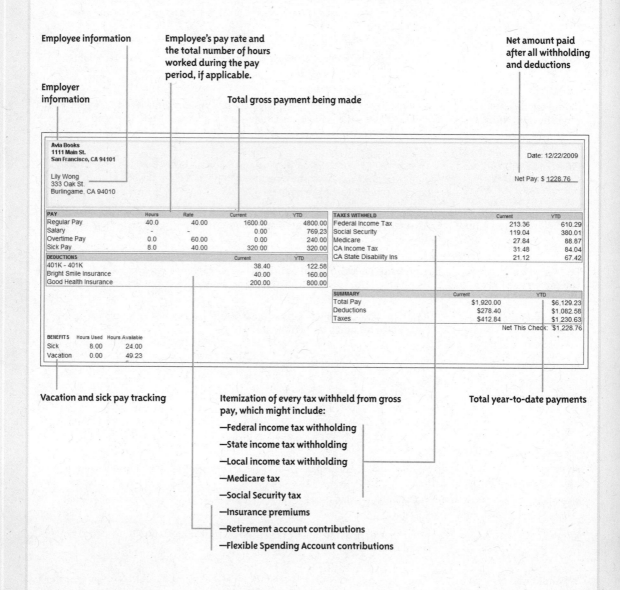

Avia Books
1111 Main St.
San Francisco, CA 94101

Lily Wong
333 Oak St.
Burlingame, CA 94010

Date: 12/22/2009

Net Pay: $ 1228.76

PAY	Hours	Rate	Current	YTD
Regular Pay	40.0	40.00	1600.00	4800.00
Salary	-	-	0.00	769.23
Overtime Pay	0.0	60.00	0.00	240.00
Sick Pay	8.0	40.00	320.00	320.00

DEDUCTIONS		Current	YTD
401K - 401K		38.40	122.58
Bright Smile Insurance		40.00	160.00
Good Health Insurance		200.00	800.00

TAXES WITHHELD	Current	YTD
Federal Income Tax	213.36	610.29
Social Security	119.04	380.01
Medicare	27.84	88.87
CA Income Tax	31.48	84.04
CA State Disability Ins	21.12	67.42

SUMMARY	Current	YTD
Total Pay	$1,920.00	$6,129.23
Deductions	$278.40	$1,082.58
Taxes	$412.84	$1,230.63
	Net This Check:	$1,228.76

BENEFITS	Hours Used	Hours Available
Sick	8.00	24.00
Vacation	0.00	49.23

Vacation and sick pay tracking

Itemization of every tax withheld from gross pay, which might include:

—Federal income tax withholding

—State income tax withholding

—Local income tax withholding

—Medicare tax

—Social Security tax

—Insurance premiums

—Retirement account contributions

—Flexible Spending Account contributions

Total year-to-date payments

The Purpose of Payroll

If payroll were simply a matter of paying your employees, you could write out a check each pay period for each employee and be done with it. But not so fast! Payroll—and the process you set up for handling payroll—has to accomplish much more.

It's important you understand all the things you need your payroll process to achieve, because you, as an employer, have many legal obligations relating to payroll.

Payroll must accomplish many things. The list below details what you can—and sometimes must—do with payroll. NOTE: The first four are your legal responsibilities —the next are optional but desirable:

1. **Pay employees (required).** The primary purpose of payroll is simple—to pay your employees for the work they've done. It doesn't matter on what basis you pay—hourly, salary, commissions, or any other method. The first goal of payroll is to make sure your employees are paid the right amount of money, on time. And you are required to have a record of all the payments you make to your workers.

2. **Withhold, collect, and send employee-responsible taxes (required).** The government requires employers to deduct from employees' paychecks personal income tax and other taxes, such as Social Security and Medicare (FICA). The government recognizes that it's faster and easier to get employers to collect these taxes from each paycheck than to rely solely on individual employees to pony up the money when they file their tax returns. Each pay period, you are legally responsible for withholding these taxes from employees' paychecks and sending the money to the appropriate government entity (such as the Internal Revenue Service).

3. **Pay payroll taxes (required).** In addition to taxing employees, the government levies some taxes on employers for each employee they have. These payroll taxes include federal and state unemployment and employers' contributions to Social

Are Pay Stubs Required?

The Fair Labor Standards Act (FLSA) requires employers to keep accurate records of hours worked and wages paid to employees. Most states require you to provide pay stubs, which can be in paper or electronic form. But even if your state doesn't require a pay stub, it's just good practice to provide one. You'll have more satisfied employees—and far fewer questions to answer—if you give your employees a detailed pay stub they can easily understand.

Security and Medicare. Depending on where you live, there may be additional state or local taxes on employers as well. You are responsible for paying these taxes.

4. **Reporting and record keeping (required).** You must inform both federal and state governments who you hire, how much you pay them, how much tax you deduct, and how much tax you owe. As an employer, record keeping and reporting information to the government is part of your legal responsibility.

5. **Pay employer-provided voluntary benefits.** You'll eventually want to provide certain additional benefits to your employees, such as health insurance or retirement contributions. Some employers start with these benefits, while others add them gradually. Combining benefits with your payroll process makes sense.

6. **Collect and send employees' voluntary deductions.** Your employees may choose to deduct certain expenses from their paychecks. This not only saves time; it can also save them money. For instance, by setting up Flexible Spending Accounts for certain expenses, such as child care or health care, and paying these expenses directly from their pay, they do not pay income tax on the dollars they use. Your payroll process should

calculate and withhold these deductions, and make it easy for you to forward these payments to the appropriate entity.

7. **Keep you and your employees informed.** You may also want to use your payroll process to help keep track of other benefits, such as time taken for vacation, sick leave, or personal leave. Some payroll services enable you to track these in your payroll process.

As you set up your payroll process, make sure you find a system that handles all of your legal responsibilities—and those of your optional needs—easily, so that payroll becomes a simple matter each pay period.

Your Responsibilities

It's not uncommon for entrepreneurs to want to do their own payroll. How hard can it be, right? Even for those who love "doing the books" themselves and staying involved in all money matters, managing payroll is one area where you'll want to get help. Because the laws are so complex and deadlines so critical, it's cost-effective to get a professional to handle your payroll or engage a payroll service. After all, if you make a mistake or miscalculation on your payroll taxes, the cost to remedy the error can be steep—often more than the cost of an entire year's worth of a payroll service.

Even if you have administrative staff, taking care of payroll can be a major time-consuming activity—one that must be taken care of regularly and accurately. You'll also need to make sure you have some method to keep your staff up-to-date on all the changes and revisions made to payroll regulations and deadlines.

A good payroll service will take care of virtually all of the payroll headaches for you. You just have to make sure you report information to your service correctly, on time, and that you have the funds necessary to cover payroll and your taxes.

HIRELearning

Garnishing Wages

In some cases, a court order will mandate that you deduct wages from an employee and send them to a third party to pay debts or obligations, usually for child support payments. But a court of law can order an employer to deduct or "garnish" wages from employees for other debts or obligations, such as unpaid marital support, taxes, or monetary judgments in law suits. If you fail to deduct the proper amount and pay it to the third party, you may be liable for payment. So make sure your payroll system is set up to handle garnishments.

Nevertheless, you still need a basic understanding of the scope of your payroll obligations as an employer.

Basic steps to take as a new employer

1. Get a Federal Employer Identification Number (FEIN), if you don't already have one. It's free, fast and easy. This is the number that the US government uses to identify your business, and you'll use this number on all your payroll and tax documents. Get an FEIN at www.IRS.gov, search for FEIN.

2. Get a state identification number, if your state requires one.

3. Have all new employees fill in a W-4 form. This shows how many allowances they want to claim for withholding tax purposes.

4. Report new hires to your state.

5. Establish a fool-proof method to manage your payroll each and every pay period on time, or select and use a payroll service.

Federal Employer Identification Form

Form **SS-4** (Rev. July 2007) Department of the Treasury Internal Revenue Service	**Application for Employer Identification Number** (For use by employers, corporations, partnerships, trusts, estates, churches, government agencies, Indian tribal entities, certain individuals, and others.) ▶ See separate instructions for each line. ▶ Keep a copy for your records.	OMB No. 1545-0003 EIN

Type or print clearly.

1	Legal name of entity (or individual) for whom the EIN is being requested	
	Avia Books, Inc.	

2	Trade name of business (if different from name on line 1) Avia Books	3	Executor, administrator, trustee, "care of" name
4a	Mailing address (room, apt., suite no. and street, or P.O. box) 1111 Main St.	5a	Street address (if different) (Do not enter a P.O. box.)
4b	City, state, and ZIP code (if foreign, see instructions) San Francisco, CA 94101	5b	City, state, and ZIP code (if foreign, see instructions)
6	County and state where principal business is located San Francisco County, CA		
7a	Name of principal officer, general partner, grantor, owner, or trustor Lily Wong	7b	SSN, ITIN, or EIN 123-45-6788

8a	Is this application for a limited liability company (LLC) (or a foreign equivalent)? . . . . ☐ Yes ☒ No	8b	If 8a is "Yes," enter the number of LLC members . . . . ▶
8c	If 8a is "Yes," was the LLC organized in the United States? . . . . ☐ Yes ☐ No

9a	**Type of entity** (check only one box). **Caution.** If 8a is "Yes," see the instructions for the correct box to check.

☐ Sole proprietor (SSN) _____   ☐ Estate (SSN of decedent) _____
☐ Partnership   ☐ Plan administrator (TIN) _____
☒ Corporation (enter form number to be filed) ▶___   ☐ Trust (TIN of grantor) _____
☐ Personal service corporation   ☐ National Guard   ☐ State/local government
☐ Church or church-controlled organization   ☐ Farmers' cooperative   ☐ Federal government/military

W-4 Form

-------- Cut here and give Form W-4 to your employer. Keep the top part for your records. --------

Form **W-4** Department of the Treasury Internal Revenue Service	**Employee's Withholding Allowance Certificate** ▶ Whether you are entitled to claim a certain number of allowances or exemption from withholding is subject to review by the IRS. Your employer may be required to send a copy of this form to the IRS.	OMB No. 1545-0074 **2010**

1	Type or print your first name and middle initial. **Lily** Last name **Wong**	2	Your social security number 123 : 45 : 1111

Home address (number and street or rural route) 333 Oak St.	3	☐ Single ☐ Married ☐ Married, but withhold at higher Single rate. Note. If married, but legally separated, or spouse is a nonresident alien, check the "Single" box.

City or town, state, and ZIP code Burlingame CA 94010	4	If your last name differs from that shown on your social security card, check here. You must call 1-800-772-1213 for a replacement card. ▶ ☐

5	Total number of allowances you are claiming (from line H above **or** from the applicable worksheet on page 2)	5	
6	Additional amount, if any, you want withheld from each paycheck	6	$
7	I claim exemption from withholding for 2010, and I certify that I meet **both** of the following conditions for exemption. • Last year I had a right to a refund of **all** federal income tax withheld because I had **no** tax liability **and** • This year I expect a refund of **all** federal income tax withheld because I expect to have **no** tax liability. If you meet both conditions, write "Exempt" here . . . . ▶	7	

Under penalties of perjury, I declare that I have examined this certificate and to the best of my knowledge and belief, it is true, correct, and complete.

Employee's signature
(Form is not valid unless you sign it.) ▶ _____   Date ▶ _____

8	Employer's name and address (Employer: Complete lines 8 and 10 only if sending to the IRS.) Avia Books 1111 Main St. San Francisco CA 94101	9 Office code (optional)	10 Employer identification number (EIN) 12-3456788

For Privacy Act and Paperwork Reduction Act Notice, see page 2.	Cat. No. 10220Q	Form **W-4** (2010)

Get Help!

Does all this sound daunting? Well, it definitely can be. Obviously, processing payroll will be easier and less time-consuming once you learn the ropes, and if you only have one or two employees. Even then, you need to make absolutely certain that you handle payroll correctly and on time each and every payroll period. Because of the serious consequences resulting from mistakes, it's almost always advisable for small businesses to use some kind of payroll service. The cost of the service is typically far, far less than the cost of any fines you'll get for messing up. Here's the basic rule: As soon as you get your first employee, get a payroll service!

What Your Employees Want and Need

Your employees care a lot about their paychecks. As you figure out how to pay your employees and which payroll service to use, consider how you might best meet the needs and desires of your workers.

What do employees want most?

- **Regular, reliable payment.** First, and foremost, your employees need to be able to rely on being paid each pay period. Their lives—rent, mortgage, food, fuel, much more—depend on it. So the most important thing to consider when setting up payroll is to choose a method or provider that you can—and will—absolutely use each pay period.

- **Paystubs with details.** Employees want to know the amount of their pay, the pay period covered, how much comes out of their paycheck and what the amounts are for. They'll also appreciate seeing information such as how much vacation, personal or sick leave they've used or have

available. Making it easy for employees to find and retrieve this information makes for happier employees and less hassle for you. This paystub may be electronic.

- **Direct deposit.** Many employees prefer the convenience of having their funds deposited directly in their bank accounts rather than waiting for a check and making a trip to the bank.

  Hint: Employees also want to know when they receive a direct deposit. Make sure you have a system that sends them an email or other notification at the time of the direct deposit.

- **Optional deductions**. Employees often want to have money automatically deducted from their paychecks for voluntary contributions to various programs if their employer chooses to make them available. For example, they may want to set aside money for their retirement—in a 401K or other retirement program—especially if you, as their employer, match some of the funds. Or, they may want to use "pre-tax dollars" (money that hasn't been, and won't be, subject to income tax) for optional, legal deductions such as Flexible Spending Accounts for health care or child care. They may also want to make other deductions for items such as stock purchase plans, meals, union dues, uniforms or other work-related expenses. Finally, they may want to make charitable contributions.

Record Keeping

One important obligation you have as an employer is to create and keep accurate records of everything relating to payroll. This is not just a good management practice—it's the law.

Governments require you to maintain all your payroll-related records:

- The Internal Revenue Service requires you to keep tax-related records for a minimum of four years.

- Under the Fair Labor and Standards Act— designed to make certain you are paying your employees fairly—you are required to keep records for at least three years (from the very last date of any employment-related activity you've had or entry you've made in your records).

- States have their own record keeping requirements—some may be longer than the federal government's. Check with your state's department of labor (or ask your payroll service) for any record-keeping requirements in your own state.

So here's the general rule-of-thumb: keep all records for a minimum of four years (from the last day of employment or pay for each employee) since you have different requirements from different agencies.

Can I Pay My Employees in Cash?

Yes, you can pay an employee in cash. But, no, you can't pay cash to evade taxes. You must be able to produce a paper trail that shows the amounts you paid and the withholdings and deductions. This can be a tricky area, so talk to your accountant or payroll service to make sure you're staying well within the law. It's a much, much better idea to pay by check or direct deposit.

Payroll Reporting Forms

FORM	WHAT IT IS	WHEN TO FILE
940 / 940EZ **Employer's Annual Federal Unemployment Tax Return**	Reports federal unemployment taxes paid	Taxes are paid quarterly, but the form is filed annually, by Jan 31
941 **Employer's Quarterly Federal Tax Return**	Reports amount of income withheld from employees for federal income tax, Social Security and Medicare, and employer contributions for Social Security and Medicare	Quarterly on Jan 31, April 30, July 31 and Oct 31
943 **Employer's Annual Federal Tax Return for Agriculture Employees**	Withholding report for agricultural employers	Jan 31
1099 / 1099-MISC	Different 1099 forms are used to report a variety of payments and distributions. 1099-MISC is used to report payments to independent contractors	Jan 31
W-4 **Employees Withholding Allowance Certificate**	The number of withholding allowances claimed on this form affects the appropriate amount of income to withhold for federal taxes	Complete for new hires on Day One and file in your filing cabinet
W-2 **Wage and Tax Statement**	Reports employee earnings and taxes withheld for the calendar year	Due to employee by Jan 31 and to the Social Security Administration on Feb 28 (if filing manually) or March 31 (if filing electronically)

Payroll Taxes

You know all those letters you see on pay stubs—letters like FICA—and you have no idea what they mean? Well, those refer to the various payroll taxes that are withheld from paychecks.

Payroll taxes fall into three basic categories:

- Taxes employees pay

- Taxes employers pay

- Taxes employers and employees both pay

You—and your employees—have both federal and state tax obligations. In some states there are also local payroll taxes for cities, counties or school districts.

The types of payroll taxes you and your employees face are:

- **Income Taxes**
  Employees pay the entire portion of their federal and state income taxes. As their employer, you do not pay any of these taxes. However, federal and state governments require you to withhold these income taxes from your employees' paychecks and submit these amounts as required to meet federal and state deadlines.

States with No Personal Income Tax

Alaska	Tennessee*
Florida	Texas
Nevada	Washington
New Hampshire*	Wyoming
South Dakota	

*Residents are required to pay income tax on dividends and interest income, but not on wages.

You'll be responsible for your own business and personal income taxes, of course, but they are not involved in your payroll process.

- **Social Security and Medicare**
  FICA is the combined Social Security and Medicare taxes. These are federal taxes.

  For Social Security tax, the employee and employer each pay 6.2 percent of the employee's gross income, for a combined rate of 12.4 percent tax. There's an annual maximum on Social Security tax, and that amount increases every year. Unless your employee earns more than $106,800 for 2010, you won't hit the maximum contribution mark. Check www.ssa.gov for current annual limits.

  For Medicare tax, employee and employer each pay 1.45 percent of the employee's gross income. There is no annual limit for Medicare.

- **Unemployment Taxes**
  On a federal level, only employers pay for unemployment insurance—FUTA. For 2010, the FUTA tax rate is 6.2% on the first $7,000 of earnings per employee. You do not pay FUTA taxes on any earnings over $7,000, and you get a credit on your federal taxes for funds you pay to state unemployment funds. If you have paid your state unemployment insurance tax in a timely manner, your federal rate is reduced by 5.4% to just .8% on the first $7000 of earnings = $56.00.

You are also responsible for state unemployment insurance, but state unemployment tax rates vary. Three states require employees to also pay a portion of state unemployment taxes.

- **Workers' Compensation**
  Workers' Comp—as it is called—is not a tax, but it is required by every state. Workers' compensation insurance provides coverage for an employee who has suffered an injury or illness from job-related activities. Coverage includes medical and rehabilitation costs and lost wages for employees injured on the job.

  All states require businesses to provide workers' compensation insurance, but states vary on how this insurance must be provided and paid for.

Employer and Employee—Who Pays for Which Taxes and Insurance

EMPLOYER PAYS	EMPLOYEE PAYS	EMPLOYER AND EMPLOYEE PAY
Federal and state unemployment tax	Federal Income tax	Social Security (6.2% each)
State workers compensation insurance	State Income tax (if applicable)	Medicare (1.45% each)
	State disability insurance in CA and RI.	State disability insurance in NY, NJ, and HI.
	Unemployment tax (only applies in 3 states)	

- **Disability insurance**
  Disability insurance is not a tax, but it is required by five states. California, Hawaii, New Jersey, New York, Rhode Island and Puerto Rico require temporary disability insurance; the rules and rates vary by state.

Consequences for Messing Up

You'll quickly find yourself in very hot water with both the federal and state government if you don't handle your payroll or pay your taxes properly. And you don't have to make intentional mistakes—just miss some deadlines, mess up some calculations. In fact, a large percentage of companies end up facing fines. Penalties are typically in the range of $600-$1500, and can be more if infractions are egregious.

You can face:

- Fines/penalties

- Back pay

- Interest on back pay and/or fines

- Civil litigation/lawsuits from disgruntled employees

- Criminal prosecution, even jail

Keep in mind that besides the government entities that check up on you, your employees also scrutinize their paychecks. They check to see whether you've paid them correctly or not paid them for hours worked, deducted too much or not funded their benefits. And they certainly know if you haven't paid them on time.

Here's something to remember: when you cheat your employees, you hand them the power to turn you in to authorities. Employees who feel like they've been cheated can—and will—turn to state labor departments for relief. If the situation is bad enough, they can also sue you. The courts are filled with lawsuits from employees who've been denied adequate pay.

Here's what will get you in trouble quickly:

- Not paying your employees, in full and on time. Penalties are severe for not paying your employees for the time they've worked in the pay period in which they've done that work

- Missing deadlines for paying your payroll taxes, or not paying those taxes

- Not properly withholding employees' payroll taxes, and missing deadlines for depositing those with taxing agencies

- Misclassifying employees as independent contractors to avoid paying payroll taxes

- Not filing end-of-year tax forms

- Misclassifying non-exempt employees as exempt (managerial) employees

Working with a good payroll provider is probably the best way to avoid most of the likely penalties. Even if you have a good payroll service, however, it will still be your responsibility to appropriately classify your workers' status (employee versus independent contractor, exempt versus non-exempt) and to accurately report time worked and compensation earned.

Options for Managing Payroll

Keep in mind that you will run payroll at least once a month—and more typically, twice a month. Each and every pay period, you MUST complete payroll on time and properly. If you're doing payroll yourself, in-house, it's easy for those deadlines to slip—business emergencies can push payroll off your or your staff's "to do" list—and then you have unhappy employees (with rent or mortgages to pay) and unhappy government officials (with deadlines you absolutely must meet).

That's why, regardless of which option you choose, you must set up a regular system for completing payroll that is truly manageable with your real-life way of running your business. Can you or your administrative/bookkeeping staff take some hours each pay period—without fail—to complete all payroll documents and make certain you stay informed

of all changes in payroll-related regulations and deadlines? If so, you may be able to complete your payroll in-house.

However, the cost—in your time or your staff's time—required internally to manage and process payroll may not be worth doing it yourself. You may find it actually much less expensive—and certainly less of a distraction or headache—to use some kind of payroll service.

Selecting a Payroll Management Solution

If you choose to use an outside payroll service—and many small businesses do—how do you select the right one for you?

First, look at your needs:

- How many employees do you have?
- Do you have hourly workers as well as salaried employees?
- Do any of your employees work overtime?
- Do you use independent contractors?
- Do you have employees in other states?
- Do you provide any paid benefits, such as health care or retirement?
- Do you give vacation, sick leave, personal leave or other paid time benefits?
- Do your state and/or city levy personal income tax or other work-related taxes?
- Will you ever need to access your payroll information away from your office?
- Do any of your employees want direct deposit?
- Are you ever likely to prepare payroll at the last minute?

Understanding your own needs before you look at a payroll provider helps you understand whether a specific service is a good solution for you.

Hourly Tracking

For workers paid on an hourly basis, employers may use any timekeeping method they choose—time clocks, punch cards, time sheets, or any other system that works. To record hours more efficiently, choose a payroll service option—such as Intuit Online Payroll—that enables you to log hours electronically and use this information to calculate payroll and taxes.

Pros & Cons of Payroll Options

OPTION	DESCRIPTION	PROS	CONS
Do-it-yourself in-house	You or staff person prepare all payroll documents	Lower direct costs; more personal involvement/control each pay period; intimate knowledge of your financial condition	Cost of your staff's time; greatest potential for mistakes, missing deadlines, improper deductions; high risk of penalties
Do-it-yourself payroll software	You or your staff prepare payroll documents using payroll-specific software designed to handle all payroll basics	Software calculates all taxes, prepares forms; in-house control of all financial information	Cost of staff time, purchasing and maintaining software; need to train staff; potential for missing deadlines, mistakes; watch for integration with your accounts
Bookkeeper/ Accountant	An outside bookkeeper or accountant prepares payroll	Already familiar with your books; can integrate with your accounts; likely to be familiar with your finances	Additional costs per pay period; potential for missing deadlines, mistakes; often requires earlier deadlines to complete payroll in a timely fashion
Payroll service bureau	A traditional outside service that specializes in payroll; often used by larger companies	Knowledgeable of updated information & data; experienced with payroll details; may offer range of additional human resource services	Higher direct costs than other options; you often must complete payroll early to meet their deadlines
Online payroll service	An online service that specializes in payroll; designed for small businesses	Lower cost than traditional payroll services; lowest cost of outside payroll providers; continually updated information & data; can access and complete payroll remotely; information easily accessible; no software to upgrade	Must have Internet connection; monthly costs; your info stored (securely) on the web

worksheet: Choosing a Payroll Service

As you research payroll providers, ask about each of the following and check off responses:

Does the provider cover basic functions such as:

☐ Filing state taxes

☐ Filing all federal taxes

☐ Filing city taxes (if applicable)

☐ Filing taxes for multiple states (if needed)

Can they handle:

☐ Hourly workers

☐ Salaried employees

☐ Employees in other states (if needed)

☐ Independent contractors

Does their service offer:

☐ Tracking vacation, sick leave, personal time off

☐ Tracking employee optional deductions, such as Flexible Spending Accounts

☐ Tracking deductions for 401K or other retirement accounts

☐ Employee direct deposits

Ease-of-use:

☐ Is the service/interface easy to understand and use?

☐ Will it integrate/export information easily to your financial software/accounts?

☐ Can employees easily retrieve their paystubs?

☐ Can you access information when you're traveling or away from the office?

Reports & Customer Service:

☐ What reports do you receive? _____
_____
_____

☐ How much lead-time before payroll due-date must you send/enter payroll data? _____
_____
_____

☐ What type of customer service do they offer; what hours are customer service personnel available, and
what are the charges, if any? _____
_____

Costs:

☐ What are the basic monthly charges? _____
_____
_____

☐ What services do these basic charges include? _____
_____
_____

☐ What premium services do they offer and how much do these services cost? _____
_____
_____

☐ Do you have to send tax money to be impounded by the payroll service, before taxes are actually due?
If so, who earns the interest on impounded deposits? _____
_____
_____

☐ Who is responsible for fines if they make a mistake? _____
_____

Compliance:

☐ How do they stay on top of changing laws and regulations? _____
_____
_____

☐ How do they inform you of deadlines and make sure you don't miss them? _____
_____
_____

Other:

☐ What are their most popular add-on features? How much do they cost? _____ _____
_____
_____

☐ What other services, such as benefits/human resource services do they offer? _____
_____
_____

☐ If using an online provider, how stable/reliable are they? _____
_____
_____

Entering Payroll Data and Payroll Reports

You'll want to enlist one person in your company as your point person for payroll—even if you use a payroll service. That person will gather the information together and provide it to your payroll service, accountant, or prepare the documents themselves. Obviously, this person will have access to a great deal of confidential information—including how much every employee earns. So you'll want to choose an extremely trustworthy employee, or perhaps have a family member (such as your spouse) handle this each pay period. Or you may want to do it yourself.

Increasingly, small businesses are turning to online payroll services, as they tend to be very easy to use. They allow business owners more flexibility as to when and where they enter their payroll data, and with good online payroll services, the user interface is easy to understand. Online payroll is typically easier to learn than payroll software and eliminates the need to upgrade software.

Moreover, with an online payroll service, you're likely to get the latest information regarding tax deadlines and payroll regulations, reducing the chance that you'll face fines. Generally, online payroll services are also far less expensive than traditional payroll companies.

Payroll process in action

How will you prepare your paychecks and payroll documents each pay period? The screen shots that follow show a typical payroll cycle from the leading payroll service, Intuit Payroll.

They also show what type of reports will be generated for you each pay period and what information your employees will be able to access online for their own personal payroll information.

Sign-up page for Intuit Online Payroll

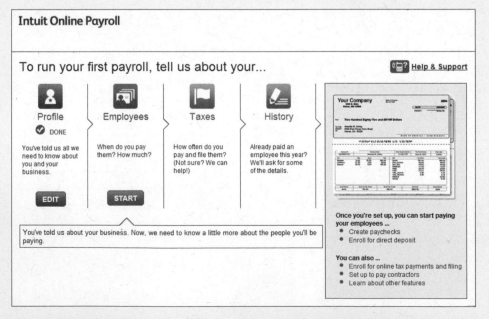

With a web-based service, like Intuit Online Payroll, you enter information about your company background and employees, and the service helps you manage payroll correctly.

Creating paychecks by entering hours

Every Other Friday

Pay Period* 12/12/2009 - 12/25/2009 ✓   Pay Date* 12/25/2009 📅

Pay	Name	Regular	OT	Sick Hours	Vacation Hours	Bonus	Commission	Reimbursement
☑	Bill Lucchini	Salaried			8	$	$ 75	
☑	Kari Steblay	Salaried		8				$ 150
☑	Lily Wong	40	2					

Select all
Clear all

Memo   Great Week Everyone!

CREATE PAYCHECKS

Just enter hours for employees, and create paychecks. The system remembers salaries and hourly rates of pay.

Sample paycheck & stub

Avia Books
1111 Main St.
San Francisco, CA 94101

Date: 12/22/2009

Lily Wong
333 Oak St.
Burlingame, CA 94010

Net Pay: $ 1228.76

PAY	Hours	Rate	Current	YTD
Regular Pay	40.0	40.00	1600.00	4800.00
Salary	-	-	0.00	769.23
Overtime Pay	0.0	60.00	0.00	240.00
Sick Pay	8.0	40.00	320.00	320.00

DEDUCTIONS		Current	YTD
401K - 401K		38.40	122.58
Bright Smile Insurance		40.00	160.00
Good Health Insurance		200.00	800.00

TAXES WITHHELD	Current	YTD
Federal Income Tax	213.36	610.29
Social Security	119.04	380.01
Medicare	27.84	88.87
CA Income Tax	31.48	84.04
CA State Disability Ins	21.12	67.42

SUMMARY	Current	YTD
Total Pay	$1,920.00	$6,129.23
Deductions	$278.40	$1,082.58
Taxes	$412.84	$1,230.63
Net This Check:		$1,228.76

BENEFITS	Hours Used	Hours Available
Sick	8.00	24.00
Vacation	0.00	49.23

Paychecks and stubs can be printed out immediately on your own printer, or you can use direct deposit. You can print the paystub on plain white paper, or send employees to a website where their paystubs are posted. Employees will be able to see all of their own prior paystubs, and print them out for loan applications.

Payroll summary

Avia Books
Payroll Summary
12/25/2009 - 12/25/2009

Date	Name	Net Amt	Hours	Taxes Withheld	Total Deductions	Total Pay	Employer Taxes	Total Cost
12/25/2009	Bill Lucchini	$1409.91	80.00	$695.99	$276.79	$2382.69	$284.74	**$2667.43**
12/25/2009	Kari Steblay	$1386.28	80.00	$238.33	$140.77	$1765.38	$193.03	**$1958.41**
12/25/2009	Lily Wong	$1108.42	42.00	$337.18	$274.40	$1720.00	$205.54	**$1925.54**
	Totals	**$3904.61**	**202.00**	**$1271.50**	**$691.96**	**$5868.07**	**$683.31**	**$6551.38**

You can see a summary of the payments, tax withholding and deductions from each payroll.

Payroll details report

Avia Books
Payroll Details
12/25/2009

Employee	Pay Type		Amt	Taxes	Amt	Deductions	Amt	Company	Amt
Bill Lucchini	Sal	0.00	$2076.92	FIT	$367.13	401K - 401K	$166.79	FUTA	$19.06
Net $1,409.91	Vac	8.00	$230.77	SS	$147.73	Bright Smi...	$10.00	SS	$147.73
12/25/2009	Comm	0.00	$75.00	Med	$34.55	Good Healt...	$100.00	Med	$34.55
12/12-12/25				CA PIT	$120.37			CA ETT	$2.39
				CA SDI	$26.21			CA SUI	$81.01
Kari Steblay	Reg	0.00	$0.00	FIT	$80.48	401K - 401K	$80.77	FUTA	$12.92
Net $1,386.28	Sal	0.00	$1453.84	SS	$100.15	Bright Smi...	$10.00	SS	$100.15
12/25/2009	Sick	8.00	$161.54	Med	$23.42	Good Healt...	$50.00	Med	$23.42
12/12-12/25	Reimb	0.00	$150.00	CA PIT	$16.51			CA ETT	$1.62
				CA SDI	$17.77			CA SUI	$54.92
Lily Wong	Reg	40.00	$1600.00	FIT	$164.36	401K - 401K	$34.40	FUTA	$13.76
Net $1,108.42	Sal	0.00	$0.00	SS	$106.64	Bright Smi...	$40.00	SS	$106.64
12/25/2009	OT	2.00	$120.00	Med	$24.94	Good Healt...	$200.00	Med	$24.94
12/12-12/25				CA PIT	$22.32			CA ETT	$1.72
				CA SDI	$18.92			CA SUI	$58.48
Total	Reg	40.00	$1600.00	FIT	$611.97	401K - 401K	$281.96	FUTA	$45.74
Net $3,904.61	Sal	0.00	$3530.76	SS	$354.52	Bright Smi...	$60.00	SS	$354.52
	OT	2.00	$120.00	Med	$82.91	Good Healt...	$350.00	Med	$82.91
	Sick	8.00	$161.54	CA PIT	$159.20			CA ETT	$5.73
	Vac	8.00	$230.77	CA SDI	$62.90			CA SUI	$194.41
	Comm	0.00	$75.00						
	Reimb	0.00	$150.00						

For each payroll, you can also see a detailed breakdown of all payment types, withholding amounts, and deductions for each employee.

What the employee can access and see

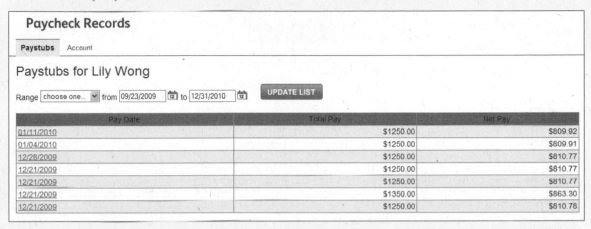

Paycheck Records

Paystubs   Account

Paystubs for Lily Wong

Range [choose one... ▼] from [09/23/2009] 📅 to [12/31/2010] 📅   **UPDATE LIST**

Pay Date	Total Pay	Net Pay
01/11/2010	$1250.00	$809.92
01/04/2010	$1250.00	$809.91
12/28/2009	$1250.00	$810.77
12/21/2009	$1250.00	$810.77
12/21/2009	$1250.00	$810.77
12/21/2009	$1350.00	$863.30
12/21/2009	$1250.00	$810.78

Employees can access all of their past pay stubs online, and print out copies when needed for loans or other purposes.

Pay taxes

Payment Due Detail

Payment Due

Tax Payment: **Federal Unemployment (940)**

For period: **01/01/2009 to 12/31/2009**

Due: **02/01/2010**

Name	Amount
FUTA Employer	168.00
	$168.00

CREATE PAYMENT   **BACK**

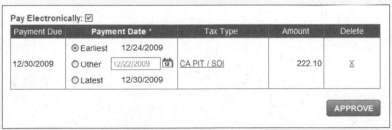

Pay Electronically: ☑

Payment Due	Payment Date *	Tax Type	Amount	Delete
12/30/2009	⦿ Earliest 12/24/2009 ○ Other [12/22/2009] 📅 ○ Latest 12/30/2009	CA PIT / SDI	222.10	X

APPROVE

You are told when your state and federal tax payments are due. You can make the payments electronically for most states, by just clicking the button. You can also print checks if you prefer.

California Quarterly Wage and Withholding Report (DE-6)

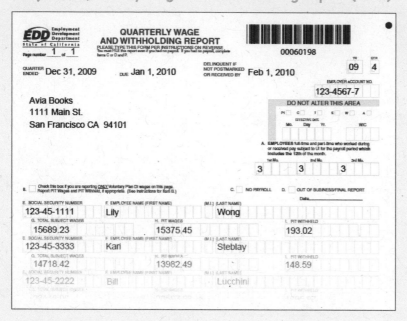

California Annual Reconciliation Statement (DE-7)

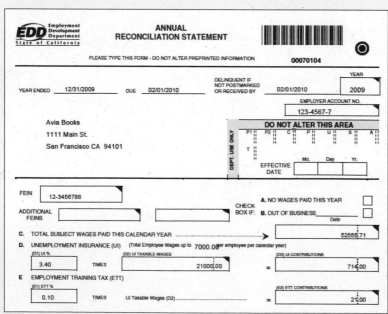

Your state may require specific payroll reports from your company. These are examples of quarterly and annual state forms that are completed automatically for you by Intuit Online Payroll. You just click to send it electronically to the state government.

Federal form 941

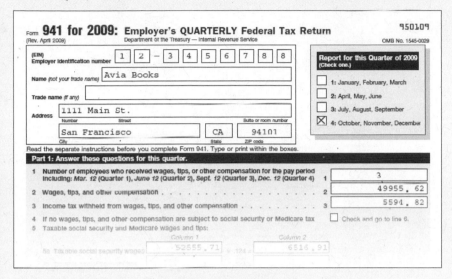

Federal form 940

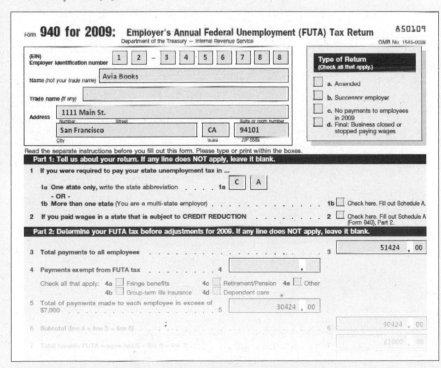

Your quarterly and annual federal forms are also automatically completed by
Intuit Online Payroll. You just click to send them electronically to the IRS.

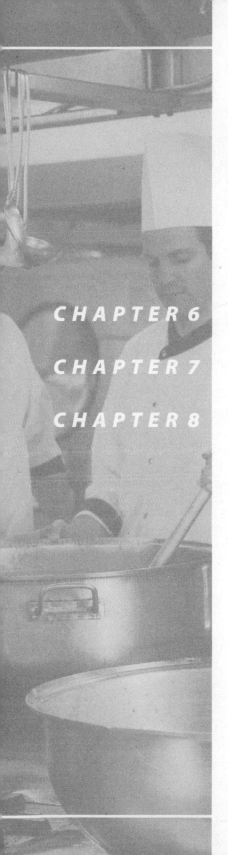

Section Three:
Your Policies, Benefits and Company Culture

CHAPTER 6   **What Should I Pay My New Employee?** *68*

CHAPTER 7   **Design Your Benefits Plan** *78*

CHAPTER 8   **Paid Time Off, Personnel Policies, and Your Company Culture** *96*

6

What Should I Pay My New Employee?

❝Why is there so much month left at the end of the money?❞
—ANONYMOUS

One aspect of hiring an employee that most entrepreneurs grapple with is compensation. "What's the right amount to pay?" "Should I offer a salary, an hourly wage or commission?" "How do I get a great employee at a salary I can afford?"

Before you make these decisions and determine an appropriate wage for your new employee, you first need a clear job description of the position you're filling. That way you can begin by comparing what other companies in your industry and in your area pay to hire similar workers. So if you haven't developed a job description yet, it's time for you to do so. That job description will be the basis of the research you'll do to find out prevailing wages.

As you set out to figure out the right amount to pay an employee, you, of course, also have to figure out what you and your business can afford. What your business may really need is a C.O.O.—

a chief operating officer who can take charge of all your operations. But that kind of person commands a professional salary, and as a small company just beginning to grow, it's not likely you can afford that. On the other hand, you may be able to hire an administrative assistant or office manager. They won't be able to provide the leadership and growth potential of a C.O.O., but they sure will be able to help you get out from under that pile of paperwork.

What you'll end up paying your new employee will depend on a number of factors, including:

- Prevailing wages for that type of job in your industry in your locale

- How difficult it is to find someone, what the labor market is like

- How attractive your work environment/opportunity is

- How experienced the candidate is

- How important that person or that position is to your company's success

- How fast you need someone

- What your cash flow and budget can realistically handle

Remember, at the very least, you must follow all minimum wage requirements, both federal and state, if your state has a different minimum wage. See the Chapter 3 on Employment Law.

As you set your pay scale, your goal is not to figure out how little you can pay but what you should pay. You want to pay enough to attract good, reliable employees who will stay with you and add to the value of your company. To do that, you have to be competitive, both in salary and in benefits.

Researching Comparable Pay Rates

When trying to figure out how much to pay your new employee, begin by doing some research to determine how much other companies pay. As you conduct your research, keep in mind that you want to look for comparable pay based on:

- Job duties

- Location

- Industry

- Business size

Job Duties. When trying to figure out what to pay, start by finding out how much other companies pay people doing the same work you need done. Your applicants are likely seeking a particular type of work and will directly compare your job offering to others, so they'll know what others are paying. For entry-level or service positions, this information may be fairly easy to find. If you need to hire a clerk for your retail clothing shop, you can probably

quickly get an idea of what other retail clerks earn, sometimes just by looking at the help wanted ads. So begin your research by trying to ascertain what directly competitive jobs are likely to offer your applicants. For professional or technical positions, finding reliable data is more challenging. Positions with the same job title at different companies may not be the same job. For example, a Project Manager at Company ABC might be responsible for overseeing one distinct project and be a junior-level position, whereas at Company B, a person with the same title might manage a portfolio of projects and require extensive training and experience. So as you research comparable pay for similar jobs, make sure you focus on the tasks and not just the job title.

Location. The next major influence on pay scales is the job location. Pay scales in larger cities and along the US coasts tend to be higher than pay scales in smaller communities and in the middle of the country. The local unemployment rate also has an impact on how much people earn—the higher

HIRELearning

Raises

You're just hiring an employee for the first time. Do you really need to think about raises? Well, as you're negotiating salary with a job prospect, they're already wondering about whether there's a chance their income will increase and when. If you're having difficulty agreeing on a salary, one approach is to offer them a raise after a satisfactory period of time on the job—say three to six months. If you promise that as part of a negotiation, you will have to follow through. In a healthy job market, it's a good practice to give annual raises to employees you want to keep. At the very least, it helps them keep up with rises in the cost-of-living and it shows them you value them as part of your team.

worksheet: My Compensation Research

Use this worksheet to record your findings as you research salary requirements for the jobs you are looking to fill. Keep in mind that factors such as job locale and benefits offered can influence base salary decisions.

SALARY INFORMATION FROM:	JOB	JOB	JOB	JOB
Online salary websites (salary.com or salaryexpert.com)				
Bureau of Labor Statistics (www.bls.gov/oes)				
My industry association				
Fellow business owners				
Job listings (Help-wanted ads, Craigslist.org, etc.)				
Other source				
AVERAGE SALARY FOR COMPARABLE JOBS				

the unemployment rate, the more bargaining power you have with applicants. As you gather information about pay scales for your type of job, consider local factors. If you're hiring an administrative assistant in Manhattan, you'll pay a lot more than your cousin pays for an admin in Minneapolis.

Industry. Some industries pay very well and others are notorious for underpaying. You need to keep that in mind when setting your own pay. For example, technology, science and health care industries tend to have higher pay scales than industries such as education, publishing, and retail. Thus, you'll likely pay more for an office manager for a software company than for a child care center—even in the same town.

Business size. Employees at small companies often earn less than employees doing the same work at large corporations, so as you try to determine the right salary for a position, make sure you check with other small business owners.

Where to Find Comparable Pay Information

So, how do you begin to research the market rate for the type of person you're seeking? You have a number of places to check.

Business owners. When it comes to knowing the current market for salaries in your area (or in your industry), it's hard to beat your fellow small-business owners. They've got real-life experience with real-life employees and their data is likely to be the most reliable for your area. Tap into your network of entrepreneurs. Look to the more-established businesses first; they can give you a better view of how the market's pay scales have changed over time. Share with them the type of position you need to fill and ask what they feel is an appropriate wage for the market or, if they're willing to share the information with you, how much they pay someone in a similar role.

Industry associations. Every type of business has a trade association. If you belong to your industry association, you've probably met other business owners who can share their knowledge of prevailing wages in the industry. But even if you don't belong, your industry association can be a help. Many associations conduct annual salary surveys to determine prevailing wages. Chances are they have loads of compensation data that is specific to your industry. Although you might have to purchase their reports, access to such information may justify the cost.

Help-wanted ads and career websites. Many employers list job scales in their help wanted ads, especially for lower-level positions. That's an easy way to check on wages in your area for your type of job.

Online salary websites. You can get a ballpark idea of wage information without leaving your chair by checking some of the Internet salary comparison websites, such as Salary.com (www.salary.com) or SalaryExpert (www.salaryexpert.com). Simply enter the job title and your ZIP code, and you'll see what similar jobs in your area pay.

U.S. Bureau of Labor Statistics. One tool in your salary and wage research should be the BLS's national employment and wage data from the Occupational Employment Statistics (OES) survey. This free report breaks out 22 major occupational groups and 801 specific occupations for the US, individual states and metropolitan areas, as well as non-metropolitan areas. You can find it at www.bls.gov/oes.

HIRE*Learning*

Don't Forget Taxes and Benefits

You need to budget for payroll taxes and the cost of benefits when calculating how much an employee will cost you. You should figure in roughly an extra 15% to cover taxes. If you plan to offer generous benefits, your employee costs could increase by as much as and extra 30% above the cost of wages. Also keep in mind that if you expect your employee to work overtime, the costs can add up really quickly.

Salary, Hourly, Commission, Tips?

Now that you know what the market pays for your open position, you can decide how to structure the compensation for your new employee. There are four standard methods for compensating employees.

Salary. Typically, salaries are paid to full-time workers—often those with managerial or professional responsibilities—who are hired based on a set amount. This is typically based on an annual figure, although it may be paid every two weeks. So a $50,000 a year salary might mean a paycheck of $1923.08 every two weeks. By paying an employee a salary, both you and the employee know exactly how much they will be earning—you can budget and plan for the exact expense. An additional advantage is that if—and only if—a salaried employee is considered exempt under federal labor laws, salaried employees can sometimes work more than 40 hours a week, but you're not required to pay them overtime. Check out the rules on exemptions in Chapter 3 on Employee Status—there are minimum amounts and certain job duties for an employee to qualify as exempt.

Hourly. Many workers are hired on an hourly basis. Generally, non-managerial workers in any field, service, retail, and blue-collar workers, part-time workers and many more are paid by the hour. The advantage is that you pay only for the time employees actually work, and you may have more flexibility in how many hours a week you employ someone. Remember, however, that most of these workers are considered "non-exempt" from federal labor laws, meaning that they receive overtime whenever they work more than 40 hours in a week and they have more protections under the law than your salaried exempt employees.

Tips. In some industries, tips make up a large part of an employee's compensation. Employees such as hair dressers, food service workers, hotel and other hospitality workers often make most of their income from gratuities—tips—paid by customers instead of wages paid directly by employers. One great advantage of having employees work, in part, for tips is that federal minimum wage laws allow employers to pay those who work for tips a much lower minimum wage—a mere $2.13 an hour as of 2010—than for other workers. Most states, however, have higher minimum wages for tipped workers and some require employers to pay the federal minimum wage ($7.25 as of 2010). If your state allows, you can pay tipped employees a reduced wage if the wage combined with tips equals at least the full minimum wage for regular and overtime hours. If you plan to pay your employees this lower wage, you must inform them in writing. You must also withhold payroll taxes on both the wages and the tipped amounts. Employees are responsible for keeping track of their tips daily. Obviously, you can only plan on including tips as part of your employee's compensation if your business is likely to generate sufficient tips to reach the minimum wage level and to keep your employees satisfied.

Commissions. One long-honored payment method for salespeople is to pay them a percentage based on the amount they sell—or a commission. Commission-based compensation continues to serve as a strong motivation for hungry go-getters. Great salespeople enjoy earning commissions; they figure they'll earn more than they could with just a salary. For small business owners, the attraction to hiring salespeople on commissions is the fact that you don't need to pay—or pay as much—until you earn the income. But paying salespeople commissions is a tricky business—you need to structure a fair, motivating, and easily-tracked commission system, and you have to stay within the law. Laws covering salespeople are complicated and vary by state, but generally, if a salesperson qualifies as an employee, rather than as an independent contractor (see the chapter on Employee Status), they are covered under minimum wage laws.

Commission-based compensation packages

	DESCRIPTION	ADVANTAGES	DISADVANTAGES
Commission-only	The salesperson only earns income on sales they actually make. You can only use this arrangement with salespeople who qualify as independent contractors.	You, as the employer, have less up-front risk.	Because the employee takes the greatest risk in this type of arrangement, the commissions are the highest—which means a lower profit margin for you.
Base plus commission	The salesperson earns a base salary—typically lower than a full-time, non-commissioned employee—and supplements their earnings with commissions. Inside salespeople—those who work on your premises—must get a base salary to bring them up to at least minimum wage.	This arrangement offers the employee a certain level of security but still motivates them to make sales (depending on how much of an incentive the commission is). As an employer, you reduce the amount you'd have to pay a salary-only worker and ideally increase sales at the same time.	Unlike commission-only and draw against commission arrangements, you have to pay a salary to your employee, regardless of the number of sales they make.
Draw against commission	The salesperson receives funds up-front against future commissions— before they've actually made sales. This type of arrangement may only be legal with someone who qualifies as an independent contractor.	If the salesperson does not earn back their advance, they often have to pay it back to the employer. This arrangement provides more stability for the salesperson and less risk for the employer than a base-plus-commission situation.	If the salesperson underperforms, such an arrangement can lead to very uncomfortable and awkward situations.

Bonuses, Profit Sharing, Overtime. Are there any other ways in which an employee can make more money working for you? If so, these powerful motivators can help attract and retain good employees. For instance, as an hourly worker, will there likely be an opportunity to frequently earn overtime? Many employees appreciate the chance for working overtime because, by law, they must be paid at least one and a half times their hourly wage. That money can mean a lot to an hourly wage earner. How about bonuses if the company as a whole has a good year, or they, as an individual, exceed their performance expectations? Small companies often give end-of-year bonuses, typically to every employee. It's a nice way to say 'thank you,' especially if you've had a good year or they've hung in with you during a tough time. You can also consider performance bonuses for employees whose work is tied to income-producing activities or easily quantifiable duties. Although profit-sharing programs are more complicated for very small businesses to implement, you can still create a great sense of teamwork and motivate employees to work their hardest for your company. A word of caution: be careful not to make promises regarding any of these extra-income earning possibilities. You can get in trouble if they're perceived as part of a contract with an employee.

Custom Product for Auto Industry Developed with Equity Offer to Family & Friends

Ryan Hagel worked on the front lines at a Boulder, Colorado "jobber shop"— an automotive store and garage offering everything from replacement headlamps to roof racks. As he installed these specialized items, customers repeatedly asked Hagel the same question: "But what will this look like on my car?" Whether they were shopping for running boards for an SUV or a grille guard for a Jeep, his answer was the same: "You won't know until you put it on".

That answer frustrated his customers and Hagel. One day, his bright idea came to him: "What if we could use software to show people what a specific after-market product looked like on their truck, SUV, Jeep or sedan?" The answer was "Customize-It," a see-for-yourself software application he'd sell to auto parts stores and jobbers to benefit their customers.

Hagel had one problem: he didn't know computer code from Morse code, and needed to find someone who did—and fast. So, before he had a product, a customer or a nickel's worth of revenue, he had his first employee.

"I told the programmer that I couldn't pay him yet, but offered equity in the company should it take off as I thought it would," Hagel says. While the coder worked on the bits and bytes, Hagel snapped digital photos of vehicles and parts to create a prototype of the program.

Within 45 days, Hagel had made his first sale of Customize-It. As he kept signing up customers,

Hagel needed staff—one that could work for pizza and snacks with the promise of a small salary in the not-too-distant future. The only candidates who fit those criteria were Hagel's friends and family. At its peak, Hagel's company, which he named Motive Marketing, employed six of his friends, all earning salaries with varying degrees of equity in the company. As Hagel began to meet with more customers on the road, his father, a veteran executive in the automotive industry, took over the day-to-day management of the staff.

About a year after launching the Customize-It product, Motive Marketing was turning a profit and adding big-name customers—at one point, Hagel had 850 locations of a major national auto-parts retailer using the product. Two years later, Customize-It was attracting investors and potential buyers. Eventually, Hagel sold his flagship product.

Today, Motive Marketing continues to develop interactive marketing programs and produce high-end photography for the automotive space. Hagel employs one person (not counting Buoy, his Black Lab) and hires paid interns when he needs more support. He looks back fondly on his company's startup, including the long hours working alongside his close friends. "There's nothing better than hiring people you know and trust to get your business off the ground," he says.

worksheet: Calculate Sales Commission

Use the following worksheet to consider options of various pay schedules for your commissioned salespeople. The first two rows have been filled out as examples.

A Current Annual Gross Sales without a salesperson	B Predicted Annual Gross Sales with a sales-person	C Rate of Commission	D Annual Commission B x C	E Annual Base Salary	F Total Annual Compensa-tion D + E	G Sales increase of $(B – A) at a cost of F
$25,000	$90,000	3%	$2,700	$30,000	$32,700	Sales increase of $65,000 at a cost of $32,700
$25,000	$110,000	15 %	$15,000	$25,000	$40,000	Sales increase of $85,000 at a cost of $40,000

A Current Annual Gross Sales without a salesperson	B Predicted Annual Gross Sales with a sales-person	C Rate of Commission	D Annual Commission B x C	E Annual Base Salary	F Total Annual Compensa-tion D + E	G Sales Increase of $(B – A) at a cost of F

worksheet: Estimate My Labor Costs

For each category that you'll have a worker, list the job and estimated compensation. Then multiply the compensation by the number of pay periods to estimate your annual basic labor costs.

HOURLY WORKERS	BASE PAY PER HOUR		ESTIMATED HOURS PER PAY PERIOD		ESTIMATED PAY PERIODS ANNUALLY		TOTAL ESTIMATED LABOR COST
Job:	$	x		x		=	
Job:	$	x		x		=	
Job:	$	x		x		=	

SALARIED WORKERS	BASE PAY PER PERIOD		ESTIMATED PAY PERIODS ANNUALLY		ESTIMATED BONUS PAYMENTS ANNUALLY		TOTAL ESTIMATED LABOR COST
Job:	$	x		+		=	
Job:	$	x		+		=	
Job:	$	x		+		=	

COMMISSIONED WORKERS	ANNUAL BASE PAY, IF ANY		ESTIMATED COMMISSION ANNUALLY		ESTIMATED BONUS PAYMENTS ANNUALLY		TOTAL ESTIMATED LABOR COST
Job:	$	+		+		=	
Job:	$	+		+		=	
Job:	$	+		+		=	

	TOTAL ESTIMATED LABOR COST	

The Bottom Line

Issues relating to pay are always difficult to handle and discuss. It's not any easier for you, as an employer, than it is for an employee when you have to sit down and negotiate compensation. As you work through your compensation plan, you have to weigh many factors, including, most importantly, how much you can truly afford.

There's no magic formula for finding exactly the right pay scale. Does it always follow that you'll get the best candidate if you pay the most money? Not necessarily. You'll pay for experience and education, and those can help get an employee up to speed faster and may mean that they'll contribute more to your growth. On the other hand, a less-experienced but more enthusiastic and innovative employee may contribute even more and cost you less.

How much you're willing to negotiate will also depend on how much you need the skills the candidate has. If you're hiring someone to perform tasks already within your skill set, you can probably hire someone with less experience because you know exactly what's required and can step in to help train and teach. But if you need someone to fill a mission-critical job that you can't do yourself, you need a more seasoned employee.

You'll find more information on negotiating in Chapter 11 on Making an Offer.

Remember, as a small company, you may not be able to pay more than big corporations or give quite as many benefits, but that doesn't mean you can't at least be competitive. So, do your research, decide what you can afford, and think creatively to establish your pay practices.

Design Your Benefits Plan

"We make a living by what we get, but we make a life by what we give."
—WINSTON CHURCHILL

When a potential employee—especially a well-qualified employee—considers accepting a job, they're going to weigh many things besides just how much the job pays. They're going to look at the full range of benefits they receive—things such as health care, vacation, retirement, sick leave, and more. In human resource terms, this is called the "package," and employees often consider the total package of benefits they'll receive.

If you're looking for a way to differentiate your business from others and attract and retain talented employees, offering a full, strong benefits package is a great place to start.

In this chapter, you'll learn about the benefits you pay for out-of-pocket. In the next chapter, as part of looking at your policies, you'll explore your options when it comes to benefits that involve paid time off, such as vacations and holidays.

What Benefits to Offer?

Once called "perks," there's a huge range of employee benefits you can offer—from the typical (such as health insurance), the expected (such as paid vacation), to the unusual (such as gym memberships). If you've worked for a large corporation, the benefit options available to you as an employer will sound familiar. If not, you'll be surprised at how many options you have.

You need to know more than just which benefits you can offer—you need to understand which benefits potential employees are really looking for *and* what it'll take for you to be able to offer them. Depending on your needs and the costs, you may choose to offer a range of benefits that directly cost you additional money. These benefits may include:

- Health insurance

- Dental and/or vision insurance

- Retirement plans

- Life and disability insurance

- Parking or transportation assistance

- Tuition assistance

Of course, you'll almost certainly choose to provide a mixture of benefits that don't directly cost you money out of your pocket but that are highly valued—and typically expected—by your employees (see Chapter 8). In some states, some of these may be required by law. These include paid:

- Sick leave

- Vacation

- Paid holidays

- Personal time off (PTO)

- Paid lunch breaks

What stands in the way of offering a generous benefits plan? According to most small business owners: money. The cost of health insurance has steadily risen, making it less and less affordable to all employers, and in particular, small employers who lack the buying power of big corporations and therefore pay even more for benefits.

You'll be surprised at how few benefits you're actually required to offer by law. In most states, you don't even have to offer sick leave, let alone health insurance. So why bother?

Consider the upside of providing good benefits:

- A competitive benefits package, especially one with good health insurance, helps you attract and retain great employees—the best workers choose companies that provide benefits. According to the Kaiser Family Foundation, 95% of businesses with more than 50 employees provide health insurance, while only 46% of those with 9 or fewer do. Offering insurance makes you more competitive with other employers.

- Employees will often accept better benefits in lieu of a higher salary, which can translate to financial savings for you.

- When it's tax time, you can deduct the cost of benefits.

- Your own benefits—especially health insurance—costs substantially less when you purchase them as a group rather than on an individual basis.

- Many benefits, such as good health insurance, actually decrease absenteeism and improve employee health and wellness.

- Benefits are good for morale and enhance the caring, family-like environment of a small business.

- It's the right thing to do.

What Should Your Employees Pay?

Overwhelmingly, most businesses require employees to pay a percent of the cost of many of their benefits, especially their health insurance. It's now common practice for employees to contribute from 20-50% of the health insurance premium expense and make most of their retirement contributions.

HIRELearning

Premium Cost Variables

Don't be surprised if your health care costs are different from the business across the street or across town, even if you choose the same coverage. Premium rates vary depending on a number of factors, including the health of your workforce, how high their claims are from year-to-year, the age of your workforce—younger employees cost much less—even your location. And your premiums aren't fixed in stone. You may choose a provider one year only to find their premium charges substantially increase the following year.

If you do choose, as the employer, to pay 100% of health insurance premiums, it will put you in a very favorable competitive position when interviewing employee prospects. They'll not only realize they'll save money, they'll also recognize that you're a caring employer, committed to your employees.

Even if you require employees to pay a portion of their health insurance, they'll appreciate that you've found a plan and have given them the option of getting health care coverage. Many people have trouble getting or affording individual plans, and they'll only accept job offers from companies that offer some way to get health coverage.

Health Insurance

Health insurance covers medical bills, hospital bills, and usually prescription drug costs. According to the Intuit Payroll Small Business Survey, 86% of respondents consider health care the most important benefit to attract and retain good employees.

When considering your options, it helps to understand the three broad categories of health insurance plans:

- Managed, network-based plans
- Traditional indemnity, non-network plans
- Consumer-directed health plans

Thirty years ago, indemnity health insurance—also called traditional or fee-for-service insurance—was the most popular. Under indemnity plans, policyholders visit their choice of doctor, and the insurance company processes the claim. Today, however, more than half of Americans with healthcare insurance are enrolled in managed, network-based plans such as a health maintenance organization (HMO) or a preferred provider organization (PPO). With these plans, costs are lower when patients use "in network" providers, or doctors and hospitals that agree to participate in the plan and limit their fees to negotiated amounts. In turn, the insurance companies direct their customers to these providers—meaning more patients for them.

Health Maintenance Organizations (HMOs)

HMOs cost less than other plans since the number of providers—doctors, hospitals, other care providers—is the most limited. Your employees will have the smallest number of doctors to choose from and, with most HMOs, they will be assigned a primary physician who decides whether or not to refer them to specialists. In some plans, many preventative services (such as annual physicals or blood tests) may be included at little or no charge, because the goal is to keep patients healthy. Of all plans, HMOs cover the least amount of expenses for using out-of-network doctors and hospitals.

Cafeteria Plans

As you consider the range of benefits, consider setting up a "cafeteria" plan, allowing employees to choose—cafeteria-style—the benefits they want in their individual plan. Common benefits on the "menu" include health insurance, dental insurance, retirement, life insurance. Both you and your employees can contribute to this "cafeteria" plan. You can establish a set amount per employee. Otherwise, you might spend more on health insurance for older employees than younger, or for employees with dependents. A great advantage for your employees is that they can pay into their cafeteria plan with *pre-tax* dollars through payroll deductions. That lowers their taxable income and payroll taxes, and lowers your payroll taxes too.

Preferred Provider Organizations (PPOs)

For somewhat higher premiums than HMOs, employers can offer a plan with a somewhat greater choice of in-network providers. In some PPO plans, employees may not have to select a primary care doctor and can choose to see their own in-network specialists with no referral. Coverage is far less—and a patient's out-of-pocket expenses are far higher—if they use out-of-network providers.

Point of Service Plans (POSs)

Like an HMO, POS plans require the selection of a primary care doctor, who must approve all visits to specialists and any out-of-network provider. Like a PPO, POS plans provide some coverage for out-of-network care, but it costs the policyholder more. A POS plan is the middle-of-the-road option in managed plans, falling between HMOs and PPOs in terms of premium costs and provider flexibility.

Indemnity, Non-Network Plans

Indemnity—or the traditional "fee-for-service"—plans have the highest premiums and offer employees the most freedom to select providers and hospitals of their choice. With an indemnity plan, policyholders visit any doctor or hospital for service, after which the policyholder or the doctor's office submits a claim to the insurance company for reimbursement. Before a benefit on covered services is paid out, policyholders must first meet a deductible, which means they pay out-of-pocket for services up to a specified amount—$500 to $2,000 or more, depending on the policy. Once a policyholder has met the deductible, a percentage of approved services will be covered, depending on the coinsurance terms of the policy.

Consumer-Directed Health Care Options

Today, several benefits options exist to help you assemble a compelling benefits package at lower monthly premiums. These allow the health care

HIRELearning

Health Care Flexible Spending Accounts

A flexible spending account allows an employee to set aside pre-tax dollars to be used for eligible health care expenses that are not covered or reimbursed by other insurance. Examples include vision exams, contact lenses or glasses, dental exams, prescriptions, even over-the-counter drugs. At the beginning of a plan year, employees decide how much they want to contribute to the FSA and you, as their employer, deduct those amounts periodically from their paycheck. Due to complex limitations and rules about FSAs, get help if you want to set one up.

consumer—you or your employee—to choose much higher deductibles in return for lower ongoing cost. Consumer-directed health plans are increasingly popular with small business owners because they tend to cost less and employees share the financial obligation. The most common consumer-directed option is a high-deductible health plan, often coupled with a health savings account.

High deductible health plans (HDHP)

High-deductible plans offer lower monthly premiums in exchange for high out-of-pocket costs, with annual deductibles of at least $1,000 for single coverage and as much as $10,000 for family coverage. After the deductible has been met, some plans have a coinsurance of 10 to 15 percent of expenses but only up to the out-of-pocket plan limit. After the plan limit is met, the plan pays 100 percent of expenses. Other plans pay 100 percent after the deductible has been met. These plans are often referred to as catastrophic health insurance plans since policyholders are responsible for medical expenses until the deductible is met, but are then covered in the event of an emergency.

Health Insurance Lingo: What You Need To Know

Coinsurance—A fixed percent employees pay for their medical care after they've met their deductible—up to their yearly maximum out-of-pocket or "stop-loss" amount. Typical plans pay 70-90% of approved amounts.

Co-pay—The flat fee employees pay each time they use health care or fill a prescription. For example, employees may pay $30 each time they visit the doctor.

Deductible—A fixed amount employees pay out of pocket each year before the health plan begins covering expenses. A higher deductible means a lower premium, and lower deductibles mean higher premiums.

Group insurance—Health plans offered to a group of individuals by an employer, association, union, or other entity.

HMO (Health Maintenance Organization)—Managed care delivering health care through a limited number of in-network doctors, hospitals and clinics who agree to pre-set charges for services. Generally, a primary care physician coordinates medical care and must provide referrals to specialists.

HSA (Health savings account)—A savings account just for health care that allows employees to contribute pre-tax income to pay health expenses. Employees must be covered by a HDHA (see below) to qualify for an HSA.

HDHA (High-deductible health plan)—A plan with lower monthly premiums but a high annual deductible, with at least $1,000 for single and $2,000 for family plans. This type of plan is frequently coupled with a health savings account.

Indemnity (Fee-for-service)—Traditional health insurance that does not limit which doctors or hospitals employees can use. This is typically the most expensive.

Managed health care plan—A plan designed to manage expenses by limiting provider options to a select network of doctors, hospitals and health care facilities under contract.

Network—A group of doctors, hospitals, and other providers who participate in a particular managed care plan and agree to abide by the plan's limits on charges and treatment.

POS (Point-of-Service Plan)—A type of managed care plan with more flexibility than an HMO in choosing doctors and hospitals. But like an HMO, primary care doctors coordinate patient care.

PPO (Preferred Provider Organization)—A type of managed care plan with more flexibility than an HMO in choosing doctors and hospitals. Out-of-pocket expenses are lower for employees if they see only plan providers, but they can choose to see out-of-network providers.

Premium—The amount charged for coverage in a health insurance plan. This is usually a monthly charge per employee.

Stop-Loss—The maximum amount an individual is required to pay in a year (often not including co-payments). For example, if an employee has a $1000 deductible, a 20% coinsurance, and uses $21,000 worth of health care in a year, they'd be responsible for $1000 plus $4000 (20% coinsurance on the next $20,000) or a total of $5000. But if their stop loss was $3000, they would not have to pay the last $2000.

Health savings accounts (HSA)

An HSA is a type of medical savings account that lets employees save money to pay for a wide range of medical expenses with pre-tax dollars, thus lowering their income and payroll taxes. HSAs have been growing in popularity because the monthly premiums are generally lower than other plans, but to be eligible for an HSA, employees must be covered by a high-deductible health plan. Eligible expenses paid out of an HSA count toward the plan's deductible. Employees can also use the account to pay for services the plan doesn't cover, such as eyeglasses or hearing aids, even over-the-counter medications. Contributions to the account can be made by the employee or employer.

Medicare vs. Medicaid

Medicare—A Federal insurance program that provides health care coverage to individuals 65 and older and certain disabled people.

Medicaid—A Federal program administered by the states to provide health care for poor and low-income individuals and families. Eligibility and other features vary state to state.

Health Options Pros and Cons

PROS	CONS
HMO	**HMO**
Most affordable premiums	Most limited provider choice
Minimal co-pays and deductibles	Minimal or no out-of-network coverage
Free or cheap preventive care	Need referral from primary physician
PPO	**PPO**
Affordable premiums	Higher premiums than HMOs
More in-network providers than HMOs	May be difficult to find providers in some locations
Can go out of network	Expensive to go out-of-network
POS	**POS**
More affordable than indemnity plans	Higher premiums than HMOs
Minimal costs staying in-network	Need referrals from primary physician
Some coverage for out-of-network	Costly to go out of network
Indemnity	**Indemnity**
Greatest choice of providers	Most expensive
No referrals required	May have most paperwork for policyholder
May be only/best option in some communities	High co-pays & deductibles

Benefits: Must Do versus Can Do/Most Do

Data on what benefits businesses offer varies by company size. If you are competing for the best workers, you'll have to keep in mind the benefits they can get at larger companies as well.

BENEFIT	MUST DO	CAN DO/MOST DO
Health Plans	Medical, dental and vision plans are optional in most states. Only employers in Hawaii must provide employees with health benefits. If you do offer these benefits, laws regulate how you administer them.	According to the most recent data available from the BLS, 60% of employees of small businesses and 86% of employees of larger companies have access to health insurance. Employers pay 82% of single coverage and 71% of family coverage. Health insurance is one of the most desired benefits—offering it helps you attract and retain the best employees.
Retirement Plans	Not required by law. If you do offer these benefits, laws regulate how you administer them.	90% of employees of large companies are offered retirement plans; about 50% of employees of small businesses are. Providing retirement benefits helps attract and retain employees. You can set up a program at little or no cost.
Life Insurance	Not required by law.	67% of all private business employees are offered life insurance. 43% of small businesses are. Life insurance is one of the most desired employee benefits, with over 95% of employees who are offered life insurance choosing to take advantage of it.

Data Source: National Compensation Survey, US Bureau of Labor Statistics, 2009.

worksheet: Health Care Questions to Ask Yourself

1. How much can I afford to pay in premiums every month and still make payroll and my other monthly expenses?

   _____

   _____

2. How comprehensive do I want/need our healthcare benefits to be? For instance, do I just want to provide catastrophic coverage or do I want to cover routine illnesses?

   _____

   _____

3. How do I feel about limits on choice of doctors or hospitals? Are those limits realistic in my geographic area? Will my employees have sufficient choice of providers if they become ill?

   _____

   _____

4. What kind of group insurance plan makes most sense for the kind of employees I want to attract? (example: young employees may be fine with high-deductibles, families most likely want coverage for routine procedures, older workers may be concerned about prescription benefits)

   _____

   _____

5. Other concerns and questions I have:

   _____

   _____

   _____

   _____

   _____

   _____

Choosing a Healthcare Plan

Choosing a health care insurance plan can be—and is likely to be—overwhelming. You may find you have few choices of providers, especially if yours is a very small or new business. And you're likely to discover that health insurance is extremely costly, perhaps more expensive than you can afford. It's not at all unusual to find that you only have one or two insurance carriers who'll even offer you coverage. However, they may offer a number of different plans, and you'll have to navigate your way through the details of the different options.

When choosing group health insurance, be sure to compare:

- Premiums—what is the monthly cost per employee? How long is that price guaranteed?

- What are the requirements to receive group coverage? How many employees must be covered? Must all employees have the same coverage? What percent must employers pay?

- Coverage/benefits—which procedures are covered? Which are provided without a deductible, if any?

- Coverage limitations—which procedures and services are not covered or are only minimally covered (such as mental illness, in-home care)?

- Access to doctors, hospitals, and other providers, including after-hours emergency care

- Employee out-of-pocket costs, including coinsurance, deductibles, and copayments

- Exclusions and limitations

If you're overwhelmed by the options, organize your thoughts by working through the questions on the worksheets in this chapter, including "Health Care Questions to Ask Yourself" and "Questions to Ask Insurance Companies/Agents".

Other Paid Benefits

While health insurance is the benefit most desired by employees (other than paid time off), they also value a range of other benefits that you may choose to offer. Some benefits—like dental or vision insurance—may help to keep your employees healthy and productive.

Consider the range of possible benefits you can offer. Remember, if you can not afford to pay 100% of these, explore the possibility of setting up a cafeteria plan so employees can pay for the ones they choose for themselves with pre-tax dollars, thus saving them money.

Dental Insurance

Dental coverage is often one of the most highly desirable employee benefits. Like medical plans, there are different types of plans to choose from and your insurance broker should be able to help you understand some of your options. Dental insurance is sometimes an add-on option or included in health insurance plans. Dental insurance premiums are a fraction of health insurance premiums. The

Show Me the Money!

If you choose to pay for all or part of the cost of benefits, you may wonder whether it wouldn't just be better to give employees the money in the form of higher pay. After all, that way they'd have more money in their paychecks, right? Not necessarily. Some benefits are unavailable or extremely costly for individuals to purchase. And if they have to use their own money, using "post-tax" dollars, they have to pay payroll and income tax on that money. Even a plan that allows them to use their own "pre-tax" dollars saves them money. And having a generous benefits plan helps them perceive you as a good employer, one they're proud to work for.

most affordable dental insurance option is a managed care plan—a PPO (Preferred Provider Organization) or a DHMO (Dental Health Maintenance Organization). Just like a managed health plan, employees can choose a dentist from a network of approved practitioners or pay more to go to an out-of-network dentist.

Other options include employees choosing dental insurance from a "cafeteria" plan or contributing their own pre-tax dollars into a health savings account so they can pay for dental work.

Check for plans that cover routine preventative measures like twice-yearly cleanings as well as basic work such as crowns and caps and major procedures like oral surgery. Tip: Ask your dentist which plans they accept and what their experience has been with different dental plans.

Compare provisions of dental insurance plans carefully. You'll find that some plans are far more limited in what they'll cover and how much they'll cover maximum in a year.

Use the worksheet to compare dental insurance plans.

Tuition

Want to help your employees be more productive and give them a benefit at the same time? Pay—or help pay—for them to improve their talents, increase their skills, or enhance their education by taking classes or working toward college or other degrees or certificates. As a small company, you'll probably want to support classes that directly relate to an employee's current job or to develop skills you need to help you grow your business. This is one benefit that's definitely a win/win for both you and your employee.

Vision Insurance

Vision insurance is another cost-effective way to make your total benefits package even more attractive to your prospective employees. Once again, check to see if it is included in your health insurance or as a low-cost additional option to your health care insurance. There are also many independent vision insurance providers. A typical small business plan covers routine annual eye exams, prescription eyeglasses and contact lenses, and glaucoma screenings. Many different carriers offer coverage. Get at least three quotes. You may be able to find coverage for as little as $50-$100 per employee annually, and it's a benefit that will be appreciated by employees.

Life Insurance

Life insurance is another option for your benefits package. You can offer voluntary group life insurance, which is paid by your employees. Look for an insurance company that specializes in businesses with fewer than 100 employees. And shop for features such as policy portability (continued coverage for employees that leave the job or retire) and waiver of premium benefits (ability to skip premium payments when sick or disabled).

HIRELearning

You're Number One

One important benefit of retirement plans: they're a great way to fund your own retirement. Many small business owners first set up retirement plans for their own needs. Especially if you are running a profitable company, retirement plans are a good way for you to shelter income—deferring taxes until later. Some plans require you to contribute the same percent for all eligible employees as you do for yourself (with some exceptions), so be sure to consider these requirements as you choose your plan.

Stay Up To Date

Employment law—and what you're required to offer—can change quickly. Stay informed by bookmarking the Department of Labor's website, www.dol.gov, and your state's labor office.

Retirement Plans

After health insurance, retirement plans are the most commonly offered paid employee benefit. In a typical plan, the employee decides to set aside a certain percentage or amount of their paycheck every pay period for a retirement account, using "pre-tax" dollars—or money before payroll and income tax is deducted. This generally reduces their taxable income for the year. You, as their employer, may choose to match a certain percent of their own retirement contributions. Retirement accounts are particularly appreciated by employees who are nearing retirement or who are prudent enough to be looking ahead to what happens after age 65.

You'll find a raft of companies offering retirement plans for small companies. As you evaluate retirement plans, the key issues you want to examine include:

- What is the maximum amount that can be contributed in a year? This is particularly important if you are nearing retirement and want to contribute a large amount for yourself.

- Can employees and employers both contribute?

- Must you match employees' contributions? How much?

- How difficult is the plan to set up? To administer?

- How much will it cost to set up and administer each year and for each employee?

- Which employees must be covered?

- What are the limitations on and penalties for early withdrawal?

Defined benefit plan

In the days when an employee referred to getting a "pension," the primary employee retirement vehicle was a "defined benefit plan." In other words, it promised—or defined—a specific dollar amount the retiree would receive on a monthly basis. That amount was the same whether or not the stock market or other investment vehicles went up or down and would typically remain the same for the rest of the employee's life and sometimes there would be survivor's benefits in case the employee died before their spouse. (There might be some cost-of-living increases.)

Defined benefit plans fell out of favor, especially with big corporations, due to the high expense. Because the amount a retiree receives is fixed, in times of high economic growth, retirement payments often would not keep up with inflation. It is extremely rare for a big corporation, even governmental agencies, to offer defined benefit plans any longer. However, owners of very small, highly profitable companies (or those whose spouse earns a lot of money) may want to explore defined benefit plans. These plans enable you to contribute the largest amount of income to a retirement plan, thus sheltering the largest amount of income from taxes.

Defined contribution plan

Instead, most of today's retirement plans are called a *defined contribution plan*. They don't promise a fixed amount at retirement, but they do require a set defined—amount that you'll contribute every year. Some of the more well-known defined contribution plans are:

- **Simple IRA (Savings incentive match plan for employees).** This is one of the most popular plans for very small companies. Employees can contribute pre-tax dollars. Very easy to set up. Low fees. Employers must match employee's contributions from 1-3% of compensation (various rules affect this).

- **SEP IRA (Simplified employee pension plans).** Easy and cheap to administer. The employer makes 100% of the contributions. All employees who've been employed for a specified period of time must be covered. To all employees, you must contribute the same percentage that you contribute to your own retirement. Little or no cost to set up and operate.

- **401(k) plans.** More complicated and costly to set up and administer than other plans. Both employees and employers can contribute, but employer contributions are not mandatory. If you contribute, you can require employees to "vest" or stay with your company a certain time before they earn your contributions. More flexibility than some of other plans.

- **Profit sharing plans.** Not just a retirement plan, but an incentive program as well, profit sharing allows employees to receive a share of your company profits. Contributions are dependent on your profits and the amounts can vary from year to year. However, your employees can not contribute their own dollars to the plan and it can be difficult to administer.

- **Employee stock ownership.** If you really want employees to feel a sense of ownership, you can set up a plan that allows them earn a piece of ownership in your company. You will need to work with a professional to help you set up and administer this type of plan.

Get Creative with Benefits

As a small business owner, you need to distinguish yourself from other businesses when competing for the best employees. So get creative! Perhaps you can provide more flexible work hours or paid time off—those benefits are discussed in the next chapter.

Especially if you're in a tight labor market, consider adding some less traditional—but highly valued—employee benefits. Many of these won't cost you much but may help make your employees very loyal to you. Also think about fun perks you can offer

that are in keeping with the culture you want to create. Here are a few ideas:

- Public transportation or parking fees
- Warehouse club memberships
- Internet access at home
- Cell phones
- Business cards and a job title
- Use of company car or van
- Season tickets for a local sports team or cultural venue
- Gym memberships or yoga classes
- Free food or drinks in the break/kitchen area
- A dog-friendly office

And don't forget to mention—and foster—the benefits that come naturally by working at a small business, like the opportunity to be heard and be instrumental to the company's growth, a chance to be creative and make decisions; to wear many hats and learn how to run a business. Working for a great small company with a caring and thoughtful boss offers a great alternative to working for a large, impersonal corporation—especially if you offer a range of competitive employee benefits.

HIRE Learning

Working with an Insurance Agent

Few things are as confusing as health insurance, so don't go it alone. Start with a good, experienced small business insurance agent. Ask other business owners in your area or industry for referrals, then interview a few. A good insurance agent can serve as a consultant—they won't try to oversell, but can help you figure out your options. However, many may not steer you to HSAs or cafeteria plans, so make sure they're comfortable with all the options and will give you honest advice.

worksheet: Questions to Ask Insurance Companies/Agents

Premiums/Terms

1. Including me, I have [#] employees. Can I qualify for group coverage? What happens if I lose one or more of these employees?

   _____

2. What percent of my employees have to be covered by the plan? Can I get a different plan from my employees? What if some employees opt out?

   _____

3. What are my plan options and what varying levels of coverage do you offer?

   _____

4. What will my cost per employee be? My total annual cost?

   _____

5. What percent of the premium am I allowed to ask employees to pay and still receive group coverage?

   _____

6. How long am I guaranteed these rates? How much notice will I receive regarding any increases?

   _____

7. What factors will likely affect my rate increases? Will individual illnesses in my small company change my rates? If I hire older employees will my rates go up?

   _____

8. How will rates change as my company grows?

   _____

9. Can you tell me about your customer service policies and grievance procedures?

   _____

Coverage

10. What deductibles, copayments, coinsurance, and maximum annual out-of-pocket expenses will my employee be responsible for?

_____

11. Is there a lifetime maximum cap on what your company will pay in benefits? If so, what is it?

_____

12. Are any routine preventative services covered with little or no charge? If so, what are they?

_____

13. What medical procedures/services are covered? Which are excluded?

_____

14. What is your prescription coverage?

_____

15. What other services—for instance, vision or dental—are covered?

_____

16. What doctors and hospitals participate in your plan?

_____

17. Do my employees need a referral to see a specialist, even in the plan?

_____

18. What if employees want to see an out-of-network doctor? What are the costs/referrals required?

_____

worksheet: Dental Insurance Plans

Use this worksheet to list your options for dental insurance plans.

PLAN	COVERAGE	DEDUCTIBLE	COPAYMENT

COINSURANCE	MAXIMUM OUT-OF-POCKET	PREMIUMS	OTHER REQUIREMENTS & LIMITATIONS

worksheet: Explore Your Health Care Options

Use this worksheet to list your options for different health insurance plans. You may want to set up a meeting with an insurance agent or broker who specializes in small business to get this information.

PLAN	COVERAGE	DEDUCTIBLE	COPAYMENT

COINSURANCE	MAXIMUM OUT-OF-POCKET	PREMIUMS	OTHER REQUIREMENTS & LIMITATIONS

chapter 8

Paid Time Off, Personnel Policies, and Your Company Culture

"Always treat your employees exactly as you want them to treat your best customers."
—STEPHEN R COVEY

Even in a very small company, a written set of policies helps create a sense of security and fairness for employees. Having a clear set of policies lets everyone know what is expected and what the rules are. It reduces confusion, confrontation, and potentially, even litigation. And there's another benefit for you, as a new employer: by thinking through these issues now—before there's someone standing before you with a personal request or an employee who's violated an unwritten policy—you don't have to make up rules in each situation for each employee.

The contents of your official policies reflect, in part, your company culture and the values your company holds. What's your company vibe? The way you treat employees, customers, and vendors, the standards you set for quality, the behaviors you expect or will tolerate in the workplace, and your benefits all reflect your values. So as you think about your benefits and policies consider these within the context of your company culture.

Developing company policies doesn't mean you need a five-inch thick book of rules. Your personnel policies can be fairly simple, and they shouldn't be intimidating or threatening. You don't need to include all of the provisions listed in this chapter. They're included to give you a guide to the range of policies you might choose to adopt—not the ones you must adopt.

You can develop a simple set of policies, listing issues such as

- Benefits (discussed in the previous chapter)

- Paid time off: sick leave, vacation, holidays, personal time off

- Work hours, time cards, overtime

- Safety

- Employees' personal conduct

- Customer service

- Use of company property

- Reimbursement and expenses

- Confidentiality and security

- Ethics

- Performance reviews

As you develop your company policies, be clear, allow flexibility when you can, and above all, be fair. Treating people fairly does not necessarily mean treating people equally. A sales person may need a company-paid cell phone; a stockroom clerk may not. An employee with a terminally ill relative may need more flexible work schedules than others. Part of your job as an employer is to constantly examine your own actions for bias. Apply the same standards—not the same rules—to all.

In a very small company—with a motivated staff—you may be able to keep personnel policies brief and somewhat flexible. Sometimes you can't be flexible—rules have to be followed. This is particularly true when a company policy is dictated by law. When you have to follow inflexible rules or regulations—i.e., labor laws—let employees know why. Is it for safety, to obey laws, or to meet certain standards? Help employees understand why a rule isn't arbitrary. They're far more likely to follow rules they understand.

Time Off—Paid and Unpaid

Paid time off is one of the most desired—and valued—employee benefits. When asked, many people identify "quality of life" and "flexibility" as more important than money alone when choosing a job. The best job candidates will expect to get paid time off, especially in any kind of skilled position. You will be at a significant disadvantage in recruiting quality employees if your benefits package does not include paid time off that's competitive with other employers in your industry and/or location.

Also, while paid time off costs you money—in the form of paying for time not worked—you don't experience this expense in the same way as other out-of-pocket benefits, such as paying an outside provider for health insurance—especially if you're paying someone a salary (rather than hourly wages).

Believe it or not, the law doesn't require you to give employees much paid time off. In fact, federal law—the Fair Labor Standards Act (FLSA)—doesn't require you to pay employees for vacations, holidays, or even sick days. Even the Family and Medical Leave Act (FMLA), which requires time off WITHOUT pay for family needs, only applies to employers with 50 or more employees. Nevertheless, most small business owners, recognizing that it is an ethical way to behave as an employer, offer paid time off as part of their benefits package. And you almost certainly will want to as well.

If you do offer paid time off, you need a clear, written policy. Even for unpaid time off, you'll want to delineate how much time an employee can take off and under what circumstances.

You also need to develop a method of tracking time off—including partial days or hours taken. Some payroll services enable you to track this, making it easier for you to manage administratively.

Some options for paid time off include:

- Sick leave

- Vacation

- Holidays

- Personal time off (PTO)

- Compensatory time

- Bereavement leave

- Family and medical leave

- Jury duty

- Military duty

- Other

Use it or Lose it?

Will you allow employees to "bank" unused personal, vacation or sick leave or must they use it in the year they accrue it? On the upside, allowing rollover days rewards employees who do not want to or need to use their vacation or sick days, and they continue to show up for work. On the downside, employees may be absent for an extended period of time when they decide to use their accrued paid time off or you may owe them a lot of money to pay off the unused time. Also, some states require employers to pay for accrued vacation days when an employee quits or is fired. One approach is to allow a limited number of days to be accrued from one year to the next, with a cap on the total number of days accumulated.

Sick leave

Do you really want to have your employees come to work sick? Do you want them infecting you and other employees? Most employees can't afford to lose income so, if they don't have paid sick leave, they'll still show up to work unless they're physically unable to make it in. That puts you, your other employees, and your customers at risk. That's probably why 73% of all full-time workers receive paid sick leave (according to the US Bureau of Labor Statistics). Small businesses are less likely to give paid sick leave, but even then a majority (52%) provide it.

It's a wise and fair practice to put in place a reasonable sick leave policy that enables and encourages sick employees to stay home from work but discourages abuse of the policy. Usually, sick leave policies allot employees from three to six days a year and often require a doctor's note for absences of more than a couple of days. You might allow employees to accrue one-quarter to one-half a day of sick leave for every month worked.

Eligibility for New Hires to Accrue and Take Paid Sick Leave

ELIGIBILITY	ACCRUE PAID SICK LEAVE	TAKE PAID SICK LEAVE
From first day	59%	38%
1st of the month	9%	8%
30 days after start date	5%	10%
60 days after start date	5%	11%
90 days after start date	9%	16%
More than 90 days after start date	11%	16%
Other	2%	1%

Source: Society of Human Resources, 2009

worksheet: **Sick Leave**

Describe your sick leave policy.

Which employees will be eligible to receive paid sick leave? (for example, full-time, hourly, seasonal)

_____

_____

How soon after being hired can an employee begin to accrue paid sick leave? (for example, immediately, 3 months)

_____

_____

How soon after being hired can an employee take paid sick leave? (for example, immediately, 3 months)

_____

_____

How much sick leave will each employee be entitled to:

—per year? (for example, 4 days per year) _____

—per month worked? (for example, ½ day accrued per month) _____

Must an employee get a doctor's note for any length of absence? If so, how long of an absence?

_____

_____

How many days of sick leave, if any, may an employee "roll over" to the next year?

_____

_____

Any other sick leave provisions?

_____

_____

Paid Vacation

Paid vacation is another highly valued—and expected—employee benefit. It makes good sense to give your employees some paid time off to recharge their batteries, go on a family holiday, or visit relatives. Nine out of every ten full-time workers for private companies receive paid vacation. Nearly four out of ten part-time workers get paid vacation. In any skilled or professional position, employees will expect to receive paid vacation. If you do not offer any paid vacation, you'll be at a significant disadvantage in hiring, and you'll likely see much higher employee turnover and dissatisfaction on the job.

The amount of paid vacation typically increases with the number of years an employee has worked for you. Typically, vacation amounts start at one to two weeks after a year's employment.

Craft a vacation policy that also defines who is eligible for vacation (for example: full-time employees, part-time employees, year-round workers, seasonal workers), how long they need to have been working for you before they can take vacation (for example:

30 days, 90 days, six months), the rate at which vacation accrues (for example: one half-day paid vacation per month for the first year) and your carryover policy (can they roll accrued vacation time into the next calendar year if they haven't used it?).

Vacation scheduling can be problematic for small businesses with few employees, so be sure to let your employees know well in advance the limitation on when they can take vacation (for example, not at holidays for retail businesses or during the summer for certain seasonal companies). Also, inform them of when and how they must request vacation days. Find a simple yet fair way for all employees to request their time off. For example, you might let them know that vacation days should be requested by a certain date so that you can develop a fair vacation schedule that stills ensures you don't leave your company short-handed.

In small businesses, you may rely heavily on part-time or hourly workers. Consider providing at least some paid vacation time for these workers as well as your full-time employees. It boosts morale and loyalty.

Average Number of Paid Vacation Days

YEARS OF SERVICE	NUMBER OF PAID VACATION DAYS PER YEAR
One year	10 days
Two years	11 days
Three years	12 days
Five years	15 days
Seven years	16 days
Eleven years	18 days
Thirteen years	19 days
Fifteen years	20 days
Twenty + years	21 days

Source: Society of Human Resources, 2009

worksheet: Vacation Policy

Describe your vacation policy.

Which employees will be eligible for paid vacation? (for example, full-time, hourly, seasonal)

_____

If hourly workers are eligible, how many hours per week must they work to accrue paid vacation?

_____

How soon after being hired do employees begin to accrue paid vacation? (for example, immediately, one month)

_____

How soon after being hired can employees take paid vacation? (for example, immediately, 3 months)

_____

How many days of paid vacation do employees receive in their first year of work?

— per year, or _____

— per month of service _____

List how many days of paid vacation employees get after additional years of service.

_____

What times of year, if any, can employees NOT take vacation?

_____

How many days of paid vacation a year, if any, can employees roll over to the following year?

_____

Can employees take UNPAID vacation, and, if so, what is the maximum number of days per year?

_____

What procedure, if any, must employees follow to request vacation time?

_____

What other vacation policy, if any, will you have?

_____

Holidays

When figuring out your holiday schedule, it's important to first understand how and which holidays have an impact on your business. If yours is a retail business, you'll probably find many holidays to be some of your busiest days. On the other hand, for many offices, customers expect you to be closed on major holidays, and you'll want to give your employees those days off. You'd be seen as Scrooge indeed if you required employees to work Christmas in your administrative office unless there's a compelling business need.

HIRELearning

Religious Holidays and Needs

When you have a diverse workforce—which makes you a better, more competitive business—you'll eventually have employees of different faiths and backgrounds. The law requires you to make "reasonable accommodation" for your employees' religious needs. What does "reasonable accommodation" mean? It means you should try to meet their needs whenever it doesn't unduly harm your business. For instance, let's say you have a Jewish employee who wants to take a couple days off to observe the Jewish high holy days. Do you have to pay them for those days? No. Do you have to allow them to "swap" Christmas or other paid holidays for those days? Also no. But if giving them a few days off doesn't significantly hurt your business, that would be "reasonable accommodation," and you must allow them to take the time off without pay or to use their personal time off or vacation days. It's not only the law—it's what a good employer would do. What if you need your employee to work weekends in your restaurant but they want every Saturday or Sunday off to observe their Sabbath? That would probably not be viewed as "reasonable" and you could deny that request.

Other days—such as Christmas Eve day or New Year's Eve day—may be very slow in some offices. You may not want to give those as paid holidays—few businesses do—but you may want to schedule those as unpaid holidays for some of your part-time or hourly workers or give a paid half-day off for full-time or salaried employees.

Keep in mind that just because a holiday is a federal holiday, it is NOT required that you give that day off as a PAID—or indeed unpaid—holiday. In fact, there are NO paid holidays required by federal law. Nevertheless, most workers expect some paid holidays, especially full-time and salaried employees, and you're almost certainly going to want to give your employees the major holidays off.

But holidays do add up quickly. There are 10 official federal holidays. If you added those to 10 vacation days and a couple of personal days each year, employees would receive 22 paid days a year—or a month's worth of work days. That's why few small businesses give all 10 federal holidays as paid time off.

If you do give paid holidays and an employee has to work on one of those holidays– for example, they might have to attend a trade show or finish up an important project—you also need to determine what make-up policy you'll have, if any. Generally, it's easiest to give salaried workers a "comp" day—or compensation day—off. Remember, federal law does not require any extra pay or compensation if you need an employee to work on an otherwise paid holiday (unless it results in a 'non-exempt' employee working more than 40 hours in a week).

OFFICIAL US FEDERAL HOLIDAYS
- New Year's Day
- Birthday of Martin Luther King, Jr.
- Washington's Birthday
- Memorial Day
- Independence Day
- Labor Day
- Columbus Day
- Veterans Day
- Thanksgiving Day
- Christmas Day

worksheet: **Holiday Policy**

Which holidays will you observe? _____

Paid? _____

_____

_____

Unpaid? _____

_____

_____

If an employee has to work on a paid holiday, how—if at all—will they be compensated? _____

_____

_____

_____

_____

Other holiday policy? _____

_____

_____

_____

_____

_____

_____

_____

Personal Time Off (PTO)

It's inevitable that in the course of a year, your employees will need to take some personal time off during work. It might be for a doctor's appointment, an event at their child's school, or an emergency at home. So most large corporations give their employees a certain amount of PTO or Personal Time Off.

In very small companies, especially if you only have one employee, you may not need a formal PTO policy. Instead, you'll just use your discretion and be flexible about handling your employee's requests for these kinds of situations rather than devising a written policy. But a stated policy is important if you have a number of employees, if employees seem to begin to abuse your flexibility, or if you just want to avoid misunderstandings.

If you do decide to give PTO, the usual amount of time given is one to two days total per year. This is often expressed in terms of hours rather than days: 16 hours rather than two days. This enables employees to use partial days for appointments and meetings. Of course, such leave is not required by Federal law.

Bereavement Leave

Most caring employers—and this includes most small businesses—provide at least some leave when an employee loses a close relative, a spouse, domestic partner. The majority of companies surveyed by the Society for Human Resource Management allowed three bereavement days. Whether or not you provide bereavement days as paid time off, you'll certainly want to allow employees to use accrued vacation or personal days off.

HIRELearning

Combined Paid Leave

Rather than going the traditional route of allotting a specific number of vacation, sick leave, and PTO, some companies lump these days together into one category, under which employees get a certain amount of discretionary time off with pay. This simplifies life for your employees who might otherwise be tempted to "call in sick" when in fact what they really need to do is wait at home for the cable TV repairman to show up, care for an ill child, or extend their vacation. You might decide to give each person 100-120 hours of paid time off a year to use as they see fit.

Other Time Off

In addition to the above situations that apply to all employees, over time, it's likely that you'll encounter some situations unique to one or two employees. While Federal law generally does not require any PAID time off in these situations, it does mandate certain treatment.

- **Jury duty.** Most states require you to give employees time off for jury duty without penalty. However, only a few states require you to pay some amount of money to employees who are absent, serving on jury duty.

- **Military service.** Federal law protects the rights of workers called up for military service or serving in the military reserves. These rights include the right to be reinstated, and to accrue seniority and benefits.

worksheet: Personal and Other Leave

Will you allow any paid personal time off? How many hours per year?

_____

_____

Can employees use PTO for vacation or other uses?

_____

_____

_____

Will you combine PTO with other time off, such as vacation and/or sick leave, to give employees a total amount of time off? If so, how much?

_____

_____

_____

What provisions, if any, will you have for family, medical, bereavement leave?

_____

_____

_____

Will you have any other paid time off (for example, birthdays)?

_____

_____

_____

_____

■ **Family or medical leave.** Federal law requires larger employers (those with more than 50 employees) to provide up to twelve weeks for family emergencies or medical leave. Some states have more generous family leave policies, and an employer must follow the more generous provisions. However, family or medical leave is not required to be paid.

■ **Voting.** Most states require employers to make reasonable accommodation to give employees time to vote and prohibit any disciplinary action against employees who do so. About half the states require at least a few hours paid leave if the employee would otherwise not have time to vote.

Vacation, Holidays, Sick Leave, and other Paid Time Off

	MUST DO	CAN DO/MOST DO
Paid Vacation	Not required by law. If you offer paid vacation, some states regulate the payment for accumulated vacation days.	About half of all small businesses offer paid vacation; 90% of big companies do. Offering paid vacation helps increase productivity and employee satisfaction.
Paid Sick Leave	Not required by law in most states.	Two-thirds of all workers get paid sick leave. Most professional, office, technical, experienced, and skilled workers expect paid sick leave.
Paid Holidays	The law does not require employers to provide employees paid or unpaid time off for holidays.	Most do. The most frequently paid-for holidays are New Years, Memorial Day, Fourth of July, Labor Day, Thanksgiving, Christmas.
Family Medical Leave Act (FMLA)	In most states, businesses with fewer than 50 employees do not have to provide unpaid leave to employees. However, FMLA laws vary by state. In Washington State, for example, some leave laws apply to businesses with only one employee.	Virtually all employers offer some form of unpaid family leave to employees who need time off to care for a sick family member, a newborn or a newly adopted child.
Breaks and Meals	Although the federal Fair Labor Standards Act (FLSA) does not require employers to provide employees with paid breaks for rest and meals, many states' laws do.	Almost all employers provide employees working a regular shift with a paid lunch break and two small breaks.
Nursing Mothers	Varies by state. Although there is no federal law regarding nursing mothers, many states have adopted laws requiring employers to provide them with breaks, sometimes paid, to express breast milk.	Many employers provide nursing mothers a private area and breaks for the purpose of expressing breast milk.
Jury and Military Duty, Voting	Generally, employers must provide employees with unpaid time off for jury duty, to serve in the military, or to vote.	Most employers do not dock salaried employees for jury duty.

SUCCESS STORY

Accounting Firm Sees Value in Creative Benefits Package

"I should've hired someone sooner," says Jenn McCabe, founder of Team Jenn, a Los Angeles-based accounting firm she started under the moonlight in 1989. She spent her days working in accounting for a large advertising agency, and later a cash-management firm. At the ad agency, McCabe found that she enjoyed working with the smaller, fast-paced operating units, most with fewer than 10 employees.

In 1992, McCabe took Team Jenn from nighttime to primetime, establishing humble roots with just a rented desk in a client's front office. "Part of the deal was that I had to pretend to be the receptionist if clients came in," she says. After a year, she hired her first employee—in retrospect, far too late, she says. "I could've gotten bigger much faster. Instead, we shared that desk for 18 months and got by with only one phone line."

By the third year, Team Jenn moved into a home of its own, and today McCabe has a staff of seven employees. She uses a clever mix of benefits to differentiate her business and reinforce the irreverent culture most are unaccustomed to in an accounting firm. The benefits package grew from a small Flexible Spending Account (FSA) to one that now includes full medical benefits and a generic prescription-drug plan. "I knew in the beginning I couldn't afford the benefits plans that I offer now, but I wanted to provide some coverage," she says. "By first offering just the FSA, I knew that at least my employees could afford to pay for a dental checkup or an annual physical or dependent care." In addition to the tax benefits to both employer and employee, the FSA "allowed me to say I don't have a medical or dental plan, but I do offer this benefit, which is more than many small businesses offer," she says.

Beyond medical benefits, McCabe looks for ways to keep her employees satisfied and motivated—not to mention physically and mentally active. As a personal fitness incentive, McCabe pays $50/month to employees that attend yoga classes and to those that walk or ride their bikes to work. She has an education reimbursement plan that covers 100% of tuition costs for employees who earn an A or B in class. Plus, employees can take two hours of paid time off each month to attend a book club meeting during the day. The same two-hour benefit applies to parent-teacher conferences and voting. What's more, McCabe supports her staff's charitable activities, matching employee contributions up to $100, and she encourages her team to participate in charity events that "get them outside, exercising, and active in the community," she says.

Team Jenn pays for employees' home Internet service and cell phone plans. "If I'm expecting them to check email at night or to take calls on the weekend, I feel that I should pay for it," she says. The company also picks up the tab for team lunches on Fridays when things get chaotic.

Looking back, McCabe says Team Jenn's growth soared with every hire she made, and that, she says, is the message every small-business owner should heed. "Hiring is magical," she says. "Your revenues will increase when you hire someone. It's as simple as that. If you're even thinking about hiring an employee—do it and do it now."

Unpaid Leave

Your employees may want—or need—to take more time off than you're willing or able to pay for. Perhaps you only give a week's worth (or no) vacation. Can employees take more days off without fear of losing their jobs? How do they ask for this time off? Under what circumstances can they take time off? What if they want an extended period of time off? For example, what if an employee is taking a few months off to go back to school for some training or to tend to a family matter (and you're not covered by the Family and Medical Leave Act).

A written policy regarding taking time off without pay will help avoid misunderstandings and conflict. Generally, unpaid leave applies to employees with a minimum of one year of service and guarantees their job or a similar job upon return within a specified timeframe. Employees on unpaid leave may or may not retain benefits at your discretion. Generally, if they're gone for only a few weeks at most, their benefits would not be affected.

Caution! Be certain that in any written policies you still clearly indicate that employees are hired on an "at will" basis and that the policies constitute a clarification only rather than a contract.

Be Creative!

If you're going to be generous with time off benefits, consider some creative approaches that are certain to be appreciated by your employees, and will help cement their loyalty to you. Consider offering time off for:

- Employee birthdays
- Well days: Sometimes an employee just wants to "call in well"
- Unusual holidays—Your company's anniversary
- Landing a big account

Attendance, Work Hours, Time Tracking, Telecommuting

What time do you expect employees to show up to work? Will it aggravate you if an employee takes 45 minutes for lunch? How about two hours? Can they leave early if they come in early?

Developing a written list of some of the basic aspects of the work schedule is a good idea for all businesses and a necessity in those businesses where scheduling is critical (retail, hospitality, call centers, and so many more).

In addition to clarifying the general policies and hours of operation, it is useful to think through how you'll deal with some situations you're almost certain to encounter—such as tardiness. It feels somehow wrong to think of an adult employee as being "tardy," but it's incredibly annoying when your administrative assistant continually shows up at 10 am instead of 9 am, always citing traffic jams.

While you want to have a clear definition of your working hours, if at all possible, consider building in some flexibility. Surveys have shown that flexibility is one of the most desired of all employee benefits. Being able to come to work at times that enable an employee to accommodate child care, avoid rush hour, or even get to the gym is highly valued. Most companies, especially small businesses, may not be able to run efficiently with too much flexibility in the work hours, but if you can offer it, it costs you little and creates tremendous employee loyalty. Of course, you'll want to make certain employees are still putting in a full work day.

Some of the aspects of your work schedule you'll want to include:

- **Work hours**
  Clarify your expectations for a normal work day. What is the starting and ending time of the normal work day? How much leeway—if any—can employees have in setting their own hours?

worksheet: Unpaid Time Off

Under what circumstances can employees take time off without pay? (for example, vacation, personal leave, family or medical leave)

_____

_____

_____

_____

_____

_____

_____

How much time can they take off without pay without losing their job? (for example, a few days, weeks, months?)

_____

_____

_____

_____

_____

_____

_____

What happens to their benefits (health insurance, vacation, holidays, etc.) while they are away?

_____

_____

_____

_____

_____

_____

What is the total number of hours you expect an employee to work in a given day? Remember, all "non-exempt" employees must be paid overtime for all time over 40 hours. However, federal law does not require additional pay for working nights or weekends if the total amount of hours does not exceed 40 hours. You may want to pay a bonus for such hours to encourage employees to volunteer for those hours if you need them covered.

■ **Lunch, coffee, and other breaks**

Believe it or not, federal law does not require even unpaid lunch, coffee or other breaks—although many states do. However, you must pay for short breaks, usually lasting 5-20 minutes, to allow employees to do things such as use the bathroom, and these are considered working hours for determining the total number of hours worked in a week. Paid lunch breaks are not required by the federal government. However, more than a third of the states have laws requiring lunch and other breaks, mostly unpaid. Check your state labor department to make sure you're in compliance. If an employee eats lunch at her desk while working, you must pay her for those hours.

Customer Service

Although customer service isn't typically part of a personnel policy, you may want to list some basic requirements of how you expect your employees to interact with customers or clients. Remember, written guidelines aren't going to be sufficient: you'll need to train your staff on customer service, and your requirements are likely to change over time. You could include items such as how quickly emails or phone calls will be returned, how customers will be greeted, and how complaints will be handled.

■ **Tardiness**

If tardiness becomes a problem, or you have a number of employees, you may want to develop a clear, written policy regarding tardiness. For example, you could stipulate that hourly workers will not receive pay for the time they're tardy (they're not working, after all). But is their job in jeopardy if they're tardy more than a certain number of times? How will you handle salaried employees?

■ **Overtime**

Because overtime can be costly—especially for non-exempt employees who must be paid time and one-half for time over 40 hours—you may want to clarify when and if employees can work overtime. Do they need permission from you before doing so? Clarifying this is usually a very good idea. How and under what circumstances will exempt (professional, salaried, and other employees) be compensated for overtime if at all? Make sure you are complying with federal law as to which employees you are treating as exempt for purposes of overtime (see chapter 3).

■ **Telecommuting**

Many large corporations allow professional employees to work from home, often at least one day a week. Companies like to offer this option because people are often more productive without the distractions they encounter in the office. It's also good for the environment because it takes commuters off the roads. Smaller businesses have a harder time allowing employees to work from home, but they may find that in some circumstances they can do so from time to time. Will you allow any of your employees to work from home? Under what circumstances? For how long? Do they have to get approval first? How do they keep track of their time?

worksheet: **Work Hours Policies**

Work Hours

— Starting Time:_____

— Ending Time: _____

— Lunch time: _____

— Break times: _____

Tardiness policy: _____

_____

_____

Flex-time policies:_____

_____

_____

Overtime policies:_____

_____

_____

Telecommuting policies: _____

_____

_____

Other: _____

_____

Expenses and Reimbursements

In the normal course of work, you may encounter times when employees must make independent decisions about spending money while conducting company business. Employees may—from time to time—use their own supplies or equipment to conduct business or you may equip some employees with equipment or vehicles (such as a cell phone or car). It's quite likely you may have employees who travel on business for you. In all these cases, you'll want to clarify your reimbursement policies and procedures.

Of course, it's not likely you'll have all this figured out the first day of hiring a new employee. But, since everything dealing with money is fraught with complications, try to eventually develop a fair and realistic reimbursement and expense policy.

As you think about how and when you'll reimburse employees when they do spend money on your behalf, keep in mind that many employees have very tight personal budgets. It's not realistic or fair to expect a mid-level sales person to expend hundreds—if not thousands—of dollars on business travel from their own pocket while waiting on reimbursement from you. One option is to get a company credit card with a strict limit for your trusted employee, but many small companies are hesitant to do so. Otherwise, you should plan to reimburse employees within one to two weeks of receiving their expense report or receipts.

It's also not realistic to expect an employee to use their own cell phone to wrack up hundreds of minutes without timely reimbursement from you.

- **Travel & Transportation**
  This is one of the most important areas to clarify for reimbursement, whether employees are traveling across country or across town. One of the first issues you'll face, especially if you live in a congested area, is whether you'll reimburse employees for their parking or public transportation expenses. If employees have to use a car during the work day, you'll need to determine whether they'll use their own cars or whether you'll provide them with a company car. If they do use their own vehicle, how will you reimburse them

  for gas and other wear-and-tear on their vehicles? (And how will you pay for insurance?)

  Will your employees be traveling on business for you? If so, which expenses will you reimburse? How much will you reimburse? Will you limit which hotels they can stay in? How much they can spend on meals? Do they have to book the cheapest airfare or can they fly business class (an extremely unusual perk in a small business)? Do they have to obtain approval for trips and/or expenditures ahead of time?

- **Meals**
  Sometimes, meals are part of the job—or part of the workday or work night. When will you reimburse employees for buying meals? Just when traveling? Only when entertaining clients? What if they're working overtime on a big project for you? Can they order meals in? What amount will you reimburse for approved meals—when dining alone and when entertaining clients?

- **Entertainment**
  Will any of your employees entertain clients or customers? If you have outside salespeople, they'll likely have entertainment expenses. You'll have to reimburse them for these. You may want to sit down and explain what your expectations are about such entertaining—for instance, how fancy the restaurants can be and whether they can order expensive wine with a meal. If you have any doubts about the proprietary of entertaining options (for instance at bars, casinos, clubs), be very clear with your employees about your expectations and their limits.

- **Cell phones, personal equipment, supplies**
  Many employees may have to use some of their own supplies or equipment, such as cell phones or home computers, to do some work for you. Generally, if this use is limited and not an imposition, you wouldn't be expected to pay them for it. However, if you're demanding a lot of use of the employees' personal equipment or supplies, be up front about this when you interview the prospect for the job, and also consider some form of appropriate reimbursement.

worksheet: Reimbursement Policies

Which expenses qualify for reimbursement:

When traveling on business, what—if any—limits/amounts are there on expenses such as hotel room costs, meal costs? _____

_____

When doing work for the company, what types of expenditures are employees empowered to make? What is their dollar limit?_____

Which other expenses will the company reimburse employees for? (for example, parking, use of public transportation, use of cell phones, meals after normal work hours, gas when using their own cars on company business, etc.) _____

_____

For employees working from home, what reimbursements—if any—will you offer? (for example, phone, Internet connection, cell phone, office supplies, electricity, furniture allowance, etc.)_____

_____

What other expenses will be paid for by the company or are reimbursable? _____

_____

Reimbursement procedures:

How are employees expected to pay for expenses? (Company credit card, their own cards or cash? Petty cash advances from company?) _____

_____

How often must they submit expenses: daily, weekly, monthly, other? _____

How frequently will you give reimbursements? _____

What supporting documentation will you require: receipts, expense report, other? _____

_____

Must expenses require pre-approval to qualify for reimbursement? If not, what is the limit on amounts they can independently choose to expend? _____

_____

_____

Personal Conduct

The trickiest areas in dealing with employees are matters of personal conduct. Does it really matter if your shipping clerk wears shorts during the height of summer? How about if your front desk clerk has a whole lot of unkempt facial hair? What if you suspect an employee of doing drugs on the weekend? What if that employee is a driver for you?

There is a whole range of issues that relate to personal conduct at work—everything from ethics and confidentiality to personal hygiene to substance abuse. Realistically, you don't want a long personnel policy dealing with all these issues. In a small business, that would frighten employees more than it would help. But it's a good idea to think through some of these key concerns.

Clothing

When you hear the term "dress code," you probably get visions of high school vice principals. You certainly don't want to treat your employees like children—and they'll certainly resent it if you try to. You should have a compelling business reason to set a dress code; it shouldn't just be a matter of personal preference. Be careful not to impose your personal preferences when there are no compelling business reasons to do so.

But many small businesses may want to give directions on or restrict what their employees can wear to work. This is especially true for businesses in which employees interact with the public, employees' clothing is part of the company brand, or what employees wear—or don't wear—involves safety or health issues. For instance, you may have a hip beauty salon and want all your employees to wear black although they can choose the specific type of clothing they wear. Or you may want all your service or salespeople to wear shirts with your company logo. You'll have to require workers in your restaurant's kitchen to wear hair nets/coverings to meet health codes.

Personal activities and use of company property

Most employers recognize that employees may need to occasionally use some time at work for personal matters—making a necessary phone call, sending some personal emails—and allow them to do so. Likewise, most bosses don't mind if an employee uses a modest amount of company equipment or property—making a few copies on the copier, for example. But if you find that employees begin to abuse your unspoken policies, you may want to either talk to the specific employees or put a policy in place.

Substance use

Issues of substance abuse can get very difficult to handle. You certainly do not want your employees drinking on the job—or even during their lunch break. What will you do if you find out an employee has been drinking alcohol on their lunch break? Where, if at all, on your company property can employees smoke? How many cigarette breaks can they take in a day without being docked pay? Will you—and can you legally—conduct drug tests on applicants or employees? If you begin to suspect an employee of having issues with substance abuse, you should talk to your attorney about how to handle this situation.

Workplace atmosphere

The copy shop company formerly known as Kinko's used to have a "no gossiping" rule. That's hard to define and harder to enforce. But the goal was to try to prevent employees from talking about each other in negative or hurtful ways. People will naturally talk about where other employees are going on vacation, or who's dating who, but you want to try and reduce office gossiping as much as possible. You're the role model for this, of course, as in so many other aspects of your business. So stop yourself from talking about one employee to others, especially in any manner that could be considered petty or negative. Even if you don't adopt a formal rule about gossiping, if you catch an employee being negative or 'telling tales' about another, take them aside and let them know that such behavior isn't appropriate for your workplace.

worksheet: Personal Conduct

If you intend to develop any policies relating to employees' personal conduct, list those policies here.

Clothing, hair, personal grooming:

_____

_____

Personal activities and use of company property:

_____

_____

Substance use:

_____

_____

Workplace atmosphere:

_____

_____

Use of company vehicle:

_____

_____

Security and confidentiality:

_____

_____

Ethics:

_____

_____

Other:

_____

_____

Company vehicle

Will your employee use a company vehicle, such as a truck or van? If so, can they use it to get to or from work? If an employee uses a company vehicle during their daily work, it may be easier for you if they take the vehicle home. Let's say you run a land-scape business and instead of having your employee come in to the office, they take the truck directly from their home to their first customer location. Of course, this also saves your employee a great deal of money since they don't need a vehicle to commute. Allowing them to do so, however, may have tax consequences for them—the IRS may consider the use of the vehicle a tax benefit. Also, definitely check with your insurance company to see about your liability and costs.

Security and confidentiality

You want to make certain that your information, premises, and property are secure. To this end, you may want to adopt policies to make sure that your employees are protecting them properly. For example, you may want to set policies in place that prohibit employees from taking their work laptops home, writing down their computer passwords and leaving them in plain view, coming into the office on the weekends even if they have a key, and talking about certain aspects of work outside of the office. You also want to instruct them on how and why to keep customer information confidential.

Ethics

You certainly want to run a business that is known for its integrity. To that end, you'll want to insist that your employees be honest—not just with you, but with customers and vendors. If employees are in a position to take bribes or kickbacks—for instance if they are making regular purchases for you—you'll want to make it clear that such action is grounds for immediate firing. The best way to insure that your employees act with integrity is to set an excellent example.

HIRELearning

Hostile Environments

It is your responsibility, as an employer, to create a workplace free from harassment and discriminatory behavior, not just on your part but on the part of your employees to one another. If you do not prevent such behavior, you can be deemed responsible for creating—or tolerating—a "hostile environment." That's the law!

Your Company Culture: What Do You Stand For?

Think back to when you started your business. What did you want to achieve? It's probably something more than just making money or creating a product or service. You probably had a vision of the kind of company you wanted to work in yourself: one where everyone enjoyed coming to work, worked hard and showed dedication, but were treated with respect, maybe even had a little fun.

When many people think of a company's culture, they think first of things like whether employees are allowed to wear jeans and T-shirts or if the boss sometimes sends in free pizza.

But a company's—your company's—corporate culture is less about these superficial things than it is about what you and your business stand for—your business VALUES. How will you treat your employees? How will you show them respect? How will you interact with your community and the world in general? What code of ethical conduct will you adhere to when doing business?

Management style is a major part of corporate culture. How much authority and responsibility will you give your employees and how frequently will they have to check with you before making their own decisions? Do you want to create a role for yourself as a traditional authoritarian boss or nurture a more collaborative culture? Employees thrive and feel a sense of ownership and involvement when they're encouraged to use their minds and when they receive positive reinforcement for making good choices.

Will you acknowledge your employees more for doing something right than you will penalize them for doing something wrong? If it's the former, you'll encourage them to take positive steps to improve your business and accept responsibility. If it's the latter, they'll be afraid to make any independent steps.

Many companies make it clear that they are truly committed to family values, guaranteeing that employees only have to work late or on weekends in true emergencies and that parents can take care of sick children when necessary.

And your commitment to social responsibility is also a part of your corporate culture. Are your business practices socially responsible? Do you take steps to be environmentally conscious? Some companies, even small companies, allow employees to devote a certain amount of paid time for volunteering. Others match employee contributions to their favorite charities (up to a certain amount). And some companies have their own favorite causes or charities.

Will you have all the answers to these questions about your company's culture on your employee's first day? Of course not. Expect your culture to evolve over time. After all, if you want a dog-friendly workplace and a terrific candidate for your key sales position is allergic to pets, you'll have some decisions to make. But, if you at least have a framework in mind from the outset, you can begin to sculpt a culture that fits you, your business and your values.

Remember, having a great company culture:

1. **Boosts employee loyalty.** Employees who are a good fit with your culture are likely to be very loyal and satisfied, reducing employee turnover.

2. **Helps recruiting efforts.** What attracts the best new applicants? A business in which people feel good about going to work—a company with integrity, respect for all, and where people also have fun. Do that, and you'll have them lining up at your door.

3. **Attracts customers.** Much as your culture can attract new talent, it can also draw new customers. When you treat employees with respect, they treat customers with respect. And if your business' culture resonates with your customers—and you consistently deliver on your commitments to them—they're going to be more inclined to do business with you.

4. **Drives decision-making.** If you've cultivated a business culture that is committed to integrity and honesty, then you already have a framework in place for making decisions.

5. **Establishes a positive reputation.** Having a positive corporate culture gives you a positive reputation in your business community. You may not realize it, but the word gets out—to customers, vendors, fellow business owners—about how you run your business. When you are seen as a fair and decent employer—as well as a good businessperson—it enhances your reputation in your community.

Remember, in the long run, how you treat your employees may be the most important thing you do other than how you treat your own family. If you treat them with respect, pay them fairly, and create an environment in which they can grow, you not only improve your business, you change the world forever.

Section Four:
Finding and Hiring the Right People

CHAPTER 9   *The Search Is On—Finding Applicants*   *120*

CHAPTER 10   *Interviewing*   *134*

CHAPTER 11   *Making the Offer and Negotiating*   *144*

chapter
9

The Search is On—
Finding Applicants

> *" If you want work done well, select a busy man:*
> *the other kind has no time. "*
> —ELBERT HUBBARD

Small businesses have a lot riding on good hiring decisions. The ideal new hire will help grow your business, while the wrong choice is a waste of time at least and an expensive, hurtful mistake at worst.

The guidance and worksheets in this section will help you embark on your hiring mission with confidence and bring qualified candidates to your door.

Write a Powerful Job Description

The key to successful hiring is to have a very clear definition of the position you're filling. Job descriptions spell out the critical duties, roles and responsibilities of a specific job. When a candidate reads a well-crafted job description, they should be clear about what the position involves. This clarity should help them figure out whether the job suits their interests, skills, and background. A well crafted job description helps you attract the candidates you want and weed out the ones you don't.

Time spent developing your job description is time well spent, because you'll use your job description to:

■ Clarify and define exactly what tasks you need your employee to handle and what experience, skills and traits you'd like them to have

■ Write an effective help wanted ad

■ Evaluate job performance against duties and expectations once the employee has started

■ Update and redefine the role as the employee gains skills or your needs change

Take the time to think about exactly the type of person you're looking for and what they'll be doing for you. Consider the following criteria when writing a job description:

■ **Skill sets desired.** Envision the daily tasks and activities your new hire will have to perform. What are the must-have skills? What would be nice to have?

- **Past experience needed.** Which critical aspects of the job would benefit from specific past work experience? Are you looking for a particular educational background or someone with specialized training? Do they need prior industry knowledge or experience performing certain job functions?

- **Personal characteristics desired.** Which personal traits, if any, are critical to the job? Do you need an outgoing and friendly employee for a customer service job? Creative for a marketing position? It's okay to include personal traits if they're key to finding a good fit, but avoid potential legal problems by focusing on qualities needed to do the job well, not qualities like age or gender.

- **Where you'll compromise.** Know if you'd be willing to provide on-the-job training for a candidate with the right personality and less experience. Make sure your job description emphasizes the things that are the *most* important to you.

Think Ahead

As you jot down a list of job duties and responsibilities, think not only of the tasks you want help with right now, but of your long term needs also. As your business grows and attracts more customers, what duties will you want this employee to perform? Forecast for your reasonable immediate future growth and plan ahead.

Ingredients of a Strong Job Description

You want more from your job description than just a basic list of roles and duties. An effective job description defines:

- Job title

- Work hours and location. Is the position full-time or part-time? If part-time, which specific hours/days?

- Job duties and responsibilities

- Vital contributions this person is expected to make to the company

- Skills, educational background, work experience, or certifications required and/or desired

- Personal characteristics required and/or desired

- Compensation (specify salary, hourly, base + commission, etc.)

- Reporting relationships and how the employee is expected to work with you or with any coworkers

The Sample Job Description on the following page shows what a basic job description might look like for a fictitious company's first hire—a person to provide administrative support to the owner of a growing marketing consulting company.

Complete the Job Description Worksheet to outline what you need and want for each position you have to fill.

Jobs For Someone You Know

You may have already identified someone you'd like to hire—a friend, family member, former colleague, or someone referred to you by someone you trust. It might be someone who wouldn't fit a typical job description, but you know they can do a dynamite job. Small businesses often grow in the direction of key employees' talents and contacts. It's still important to create a job description. Look at your greatest needs and see which they're best suited for. This can be a collaborative process. A good job description helps both of you understand the scope of the job and what is expected of them.

sample document: **Sample Job Description**

Job Title: Office Coordinator
Reports to: xyzMarketing.com President/owner
Hours & Location: Full-time 9:00-5:30 Monday-Friday, downtown Palo Alto

Job Responsibilities
- Manages all client-facing interactions including answering phones in a professional manner.
- Serves as first point of contact with clients, vendors and partners.
- Handles routine client questions, especially when the President is out of the office.
- Collects email questions and comments from the company's Web site daily, answers routine inquiries.
- Assembles materials and documents for customer proposals.
- Coordinates scheduling of client meetings.
- Monitors status of all office supplies, equipment and critical materials, and places orders as needed.
- Word processing, data entry, filing.

Vital contributions
- Ensures that all callers and visitors are greeted warmly and that their inquiries are handled promptly.
- Reinforces the company's professional image and client-centered culture.
- Provides efficient administrative support to company President to free her from routine tasks.

Required Skills, Education and Certifications
- Proficient using both Mac and Windows computers, specifically Microsoft Office applications, especially Microsoft Word and Outlook, Web browsers, and email applications.
- Familiarity with essential office machines: printer, fax, copier, etc.
- High school diploma, GED or equivalent required; college degree preferred.
- Prior administrative office experience preferred.

Other Skills and Abilities Desired
- Effective communicator and excellent telephone manner.
- Comfortable in a small, highly collaborative environment.
- Motivated individual with a knack for solving problems.

Salary Range: $25,000 - $35,000, based on experience. Health and dental insurance.

worksheet: **Write a Job Description**

Job title: _____

Reports to: _____

Hours/location: _____

Job duties and responsibilities:

1. _____

2. _____

3. _____

4. _____

5. _____

6. _____

7. _____

8. _____

Vital contributions and outcomes of the position:

_____

_____

Required qualifications of candidate (specific skills, education, years of experience, certifications, etc.):

_____

Other desired skills, including personal characteristics: _____

_____

Salary/hourly wage, benefits, other compensation: _____

_____

Craft a Compelling Help Wanted Ad

When you start your search for job candidates, remember to aim for quality, not quantity. You want just enough of the *right kind* of candidates, and not an inbox full of responses that don't meet your needs. To that end, the more specific and clear you can be in your help wanted ad, the better the quality of your respondents will be.

You already have the makings of a help wanted ad in your job description. Now just put yourself in the shoes of someone who has no current knowledge of your company or the kind of help you need. Write an ad that brings your need to life and clearly describes what you're looking for.

Here's one difference between your job description and your help wanted ad: go light on the personal characteristics desired. It's good to define what you're looking for and know what personality traits you'd like to see, but listing "go-getter" or "organized" in an ad is much like asking a leading question—you'll get the response you're looking for even if it's not a quality the candidates themselves really have. Better to focus on objective skills and qualifications at this phase, then ask questions during the interview process that help you determine if the candidate fits well personality-wise.

If you offer good benefits—especially health insurance (even if employees have to pay a portion of their premium)—list those in your ad. Many candidates look for jobs that offer health insurance, and the fact that you do makes you a more attractive option.

Show Some Company Culture

By showing some personality in your ad, you will increase your chances of attracting candidates who fit well with you and your business. Even if you're hiring employee #1, think of ways to describe the kind of company "culture" you want to create. Will the office have a very professional atmosphere or a more relaxed one? Should the worker expect a collaborative, team-oriented environment or will they work more independently? If you have one, perhaps you would like to include your company's mission statement. Anything you can do to illuminate the type of working environment and company culture helps you increase your chances of finding the right employee. A good personality fit matters to any employer, but it's especially important for small business owners, where all employees interact every day.

How can you inject life into even a seemingly low-profile role? Well, if an administrative job entails a wide variety of tasks, you might use the wording "Duties from the sublime to the ridiculous" or state, "Some days you'll feel like a rock star; other days you'll feel like the rock star's chauffeur."

For example, SUBWAY® doesn't post signs seeking "sandwich makers," they advertise for "Sandwich Artists." In those two words, they indicate they hope to find more than just a typical fast food worker.

Based on the fictional Office Coordinator job description in the Sample Job Description in this

HIRELearning

Employment Agencies, Recruiters, "Headhunters"

Depending on the type of job opening you're trying to fill and your time constraints, paying an employment agency or a recruiting company—typically referred to as a "headhunter"—might be worth the expense. Employment agencies can run ads and screen applicants for you, and they may have a candidate pool from which to draw. Headhunters may reach out to individuals who have the job qualifications you're looking for but who are currently employed and aren't actively job hunting. Expect to pay 20-35 percent of the cost of the new recruit's annual salary. But, for high level positions in specific industries, the cost is worth the time you save and talent you find.

chapter and the corporate culture you want to convey, you could take two different approaches as shown in the sample want ads on the next page.

If you have a fun, casual work environment, a clever job title, or unusual benefits that will appeal to appropriate potential applicants, put those descriptions in your ad. For example if you allow employees to bring their dogs to work: "a dog-friendly and human-friendly office"—or provide free food frequently: "frequent Friday pizza lunches on us"—including such perks in your job description makes your ad stand out. Maybe this approach isn't your style. Don't force or fake anything. Just remember, the more thought you put into how you represent your business in the ad, the more likely you will attract candidates who can fit into the culture you're developing. After all, this is *your* company. Express yourself.

What *Not* to Put in a Want Ad

Almost as important as figuring out what to put in a help wanted ad is figuring out what you should leave out. You want to attract the right potential applicants, and not turn off good candidates by including information that's irrelevant. Moreover, you want to make sure you stay well within the law when you advertise your job opening.

It's important to remember that you can not discriminate in hiring on the basis of many "covered classes," (such as race, sex, national origin, age), so you want to *absolutely* avoid any language that might imply you're actually or subtly discriminating.

What kinds of things should you leave OUT of your help wanted ad:

■ Duties that will take up little of your employee's time and that are not critical to the job.

■ Highly subjective personality traits that are not critical to the job, such as "We really want someone who isn't moody or whiny."

■ Any mention of race, gender, nationality, or marital status, or any other discriminatory attribute.

■ Language that could be considered discriminatory, such as "seeking energetic, college-age candidates," "need individuals with no family responsibilities," "only want native speakers of English."

■ Specific details on benefits if you have not yet ironed out your benefits plan or if the benefits will be reduced or eliminated soon.

■ Any promises or hints of job security.

Should You Include Salary on Your Want Ad?

You may not want to list the salary or hourly pay you're offering in your ad, and plenty of people don't, especially for professional or higher-level positions. But if you're absolutely certain of the salary range you're willing to pay, you'll get more suitable responses if you include that information.

Listing a Salary in Your Want Ad— Why or Why Not?

WHY	WHY NOT
Without a salary range, some qualified applicants may not apply	Gives you more negotiating room once you see the applicant
With some online search engines, jobs without salaries won't appear in results	You won't pay more than an applicant would have asked for
Salaries let seekers know how junior or senior the job is	Prevents existing staff from knowing what you're offering
Get more appropriate candidates; avoids sifting through candidates who won't consider your salary range	Prevents competitors from knowing what you pay

sample document: Two Approaches to a Help Wanted Ad

Buttoned-Down

Office Coordinator

- A rapidly growing, small marketing firm needs an Office Coordinator to provide a wide range of administrative support duties. Job duties include, but are not limited to, managing day-to-day client interactions including answering phones and greeting visitors, scheduling client meetings, assembling materials for proposals, monitoring office equipment and supplies.

- Must have an engaging attitude with good people skills. Will be in charge of office, so good organizational skills are necessary, and the ability to work unsupervised is essential.

- Must be proficient using both Mac and Windows computers, Microsoft Office applications, especially Microsoft Word and Outlook, Web browsers, and email applications.

- Must have worked with essential office machines: printer, fax, copier, etc.

- High school diploma, GED or equivalent required; college degree preferred.

- Prior administrative office experience preferred.

Salary range: $25,000-$35,000 depending on experience. Health and dental insurance offered.

Full-time. Downtown Palo Alto.

Send your resume to jobs@xyzMarketing.com

No calls. Email only.

Fun and Casual

Office Wizard

Our small but growing marketing firm can't keep up with it all. We need an Office Wizard to wave a magic wand and bring it all together! So, what's an Office Wizard? Someone with top-notch organization skills. Someone who can answer phones and greet clients with an engaging personality. Someone who can assemble materials for customer proposals and always get it right. Someone who can make sure that the office has everything it needs to run smoothly—equipment, supplies, and the like. And most importantly, someone who can provide all the administrative support our company owner/CEO needs—and can do it without supervision. And can do all this all at once—and much more!

So, do you have what it takes to be our Office Wizard? If so, you'll be proficient on both PC and Mac computers, be familiar with Microsoft Office applications, especially Word and Outlook. Have at least a High School degree or GED—but we'd prefer a college degree.

We're offering $25-000-$35,000, depending on your experience. And we also have a company health and dental insurance plan.

Full-time. Downtown Palo Alto.

If this description fits, then we want to talk to you! Send your resume to jobs @xyzMarketing. com.

Please, no calls. Just send us your qualifications. If we see a fit, we'll call you. We promise.

worksheet: Plan Your Want Ad

Job Title: _____

What are the work hours and location? Is the position full-time or part-time? _____
_____

What are the most important job duties and responsibilities? List and describe them. _____
_____
_____

What are the top skills required to do the job successfully? Required education, experience, certifications?
_____
_____

Which aspects of your company, mission or corporate culture are important for candidates to know?
_____
_____

What unusual or appealing aspects of your company and/or job opening will make your position more
appealing to candidates? What makes you stand out from others?
_____
_____

How do you want applicants to respond (email, online, in-person, phone, fax)? What specifically do you want
them to send (resume, cover letter, work samples, references)?
_____

Do you want to include salary and/or benefits information? If so, list here. Are there any interesting, unusual
benefits or compensation?
_____
_____

Other points to mention in ads: _____
_____

Choose the Perfect Place for Your Ad

Once you've come up with a compelling help wanted ad and job description, you need to get the word out to appropriate job seekers. Where will you find the right type of person to fill your job? How will you let them know you have a job opening?

Once, the choices for placing a help wanted ad were slim: paying for ads in local newspaper classifieds, putting a help wanted sign in the window, and letting a few people know you were looking. Other than that, there weren't many affordable options for small businesses. Oh, how times have changed! Of course, most job-seekers turn to the Internet. But there are plenty of Internet job sites. Which sites do you choose? And there are many other, sometimes more effective methods of finding appropriate candidates. So don't throw all of your recruiting eggs into one basket.

Your goal is to attract many qualified, good candidates and find the best fit for you. It would be a shame if your perfect candidate was desperately seeking a job but never heard of your job opening. So expose your open position to a broad audience to get a solid pool of candidates.

One of the easiest places to start your search is through those closest to you—other business-people in your networking groups, colleagues in your industry, friends and family. Why not notify your Facebook friends or people who follow you on Twitter? You can also send out a simple email—including your help wanted description—to people on your contact list. Ask them to spread the word to their own networks. Word of mouth is a great way to get candidates with recommendations you can trust.

Don't forget to speak with your vendors, consultants, and employees. If you already have employees, definitely ask them to recommend any friends or family members. Often, good employees have capable friends as well. And tell your consultants or service providers, such as attorneys, accountants, website developers.

And the good news with word-of-mouth methods is that they're free!

Where to Advertise Your Job Opening

To get the broadest applicant pool, you need to expand beyond your personal network. That typically means advertising your job opening. But help wanted ads can get expensive. They're often the most expensive ads on websites and in industry publications.

Carefully think through whether the venue you choose will attract candidates at the right level of expertise or experience. This may differ depending on what type of job opening you have. For instance, if you have a clothing boutique and you're looking for an entry-level retail clerk, you might want to advertise in your local Craigslist or local online job website, and put a sign in your window. But if you're looking for an experienced clothing buyer, you're likely to have much better luck placing an ad on an apparel industry trade association website.

The list below outlines most of the major places to post your help wanted ad and spread the word about your job opening.

- **Your company website**—A "Join Our Team" section has the potential to attract candidates already familiar with your business. Also, consider including your web address in your help wanted ads posted elsewhere, especially if your website does a particularly good job of "selling" your company.

- **Craigslist**—Craigslist.org is a mostly free online marketplace where you can sell your old golf clubs, buy a dog, or look for a job. Posting a job opening on craigslist, in most major U.S. markets costs $25, and $75 for the San Francisco Bay Area. It's one of the most cost-effective options available today and appeals to a broad audience.

■ **General career websites.** The best-known of the job-hunting sites such as Yahoo HotJobs, Monster.com or CareerBuilder.com are likely to attract a large number of job hunters. Because these sites have a large reach, they often command higher fees than some other options.

■ **Local job career websites.** Regional efforts, sometimes run by the local newspaper, offer a more targeted and perhaps more affordable option for small companies. Jobing.com, for example, contains sites specifically for many metro areas, such as *Dallas.Jobing.com.*

■ **LinkedIn.** This social networking site, aimed at business users for business purposes, has become a favorite for "head hunters"—employment agencies looking for currently-employed individuals for clients with job openings. It's also become a good place to post openings, especially for professional and technical jobs. You can also cross-check applicant's resumes against information they've posted online.

■ **Other social media sites.** If you're on Facebook, MySpace or Twitter, don't be afraid to let people know you're looking to hire.

■ **Industry-specific sites.** Many industry associations or trade journals run websites that accept job opening listings. If you need to find candidates with experience in your industry, especially if you're willing to relocate them from other geographic areas, these industry job listing sites are a good bet. Examples include Mediabistro.com for media professionals or Idealist.org for people that want to get into the non-profit world. Search for a resource in your industry.

■ **Industry associations.** Your industry association, even a local chapter, may have a newsletter or other vehicle for communicating your opening to potential candidates. And be sure to tell people at your trade association meetings.

■ **College career centers.** Most colleges, including private and career colleges, maintain career centers to help soon-to-graduate students find career

jobs and current students to find part-time work. These can be a great place to find entry-level and part-time workers. List your job with them.

■ **Sign in the window.** Don't forget the old, tried-and-true method of putting up a "help wanted" sign. This works especially well for retail and hospitality establishments looking to hire local help.

■ **Newspapers.** Use large metro or local newspapers ads for non-professional jobs or for jobs appealing to older workers. Neighborhood newspapers can be effective for retail and service jobs in your specific geographic area.

■ **Unemployment offices.** Individuals who've been laid off from their jobs typically interact regularly with these government agencies.

To find that jewel of an employee who's out there waiting for you, just remember to get the word out to as many potential candidates as you can—without blowing your advertising budget or burying your desk with unqualified resumes.

Places to Find Job Candidates

Check off the places that are best suited for your job hunt:

- ☐ Your company website
- ☐ Your personal network
- ☐ Current or former employees
- ☐ Craigslist
- ☐ Career websites
- ☐ LinkedIn, other business websites
- ☐ Social media sites: MySpace, Twitter, Facebook, etc.
- ☐ Industry association/industry websites
- ☐ Career centers at schools/colleges/universities
- ☐ Signs in window
- ☐ Newspapers
- ☐ Unemployment offices
- ☐ Other referral sources

The Application Process

Once you have figured out what you want to say in your help wanted ad and where you'll place it, you have to determine how you'll actually manage the process of receiving resumes or applications. You want to let applicants know exactly what process they need to follow to contact you. In your ad, make sure you list exactly what you want from applicants (Resumes? Cover letters? Work samples?) and how they are to contact you.

The first thing you'll have to decide is *where* you want potential candidates to send you their applications or resumes. Do you want to only get applications via email? Can applicants stop by and fill out an application and leave it in person? Can they mail or fax their resumes? Should they fill out a form on your website? To a large extent, where you choose to have them respond should relate to where you've placed your help wanted ads. If you're using online job sites, most candidates are going to want to send you their resumes via email. If you've got a sign in the window, they're likely to come in person.

Email is typically the best choice. If possible, set up a dedicated email address, such as jobs@yourcompany.com. That way, your own email address won't be on public career websites. It's also polite and efficient to set up an "auto-responder" to acknowledge that you've received the resume or application. Just say something like, "Thank you for your interest in the job at XYZ Marketing company. We have received your application and will be going through it soon. We'll get in touch with you if your qualifications seem to be a good fit with our needs." That way, you don't have to respond personally to those who are not appropriate for your position.

If you're going to need a lot of employees and have a lot of employee turnover—let's say you're operating a fast food restaurant or coffee house—create an ongoing recruitment campaign. Keep a sign up in your place of business saying that you're always looking for eager job applicants and have a stack of applications on hand. Put and keep a notice on your website. Continually remind friends and family that you're always hiring.

Privacy Laws Federal law requires you to guard the personal information you collect from job applicants—whether they give you this information on an application form or in a resume. This is particularly true with data such as someone's Social Security number, but you must be careful even with their addresses and phone numbers. As you collect information from applicants, keep the applications or resumes in a secure, out-of-plain-sight location—don't leave them out on your desk! And once you've made your decision, you need to shred or delete applications from the candidates you didn't hire. If you're saving some resumes for potential future openings, keep these in a secure, private spot.

Job Applications

In many types of businesses, job candidates are much less likely to submit resumes. Instead, you're going to want to ask them to fill out a job application. This is particularly true for certain industries, such as hospitality, retail, and service workers. It's not realistic to expect a 19-year-old who's applying to wait tables at your café or to clerk at your boutique to come in with a professional-looking resume.

For these types of jobs, many applicants will stop by your place of business, asking if you have any job openings. This is particularly true if you put a help wanted sign in your window or in the front of your business. Even if you run a help wanted ad, you'll probably ask interested candidates who respond to your ad to stop by and pick up an application form. So you'll want to have a stack of application forms handy. If you don't have a place of business yet, you can email them a copy of an application form and ask that they bring or mail you their completed job application form.

Even if yours is the type of job where asking for—and receiving—resumes is common, you may also want candidates to complete a job application form. Doing so makes it certain that you ask for—and get—the same information from every applicant. You may be able to get more details than you would get in a resume that a clever applicant has crafted just for your position.

Sub Shop Owner Finds Sweet Spot with Part-Timers

Charles Garrison had spent enough time on airplanes away from his wife, Julie, and their two children. He wanted off the corporate treadmill and sought an alternative to his fast-lane, ladder-climbing life in Tennessee. One look at the Sonoran Desert, and the Garrisons discovered their refuge and new home—and the location for their new business: The Bad Donkey Sub, Salad and Pizza Co., in Carefree, Arizona.

Charles, with absolutely no restaurant experience, laid the groundwork for The Bad Donkey. "In my corporate life, I was in high-level positions doing planning and creating business models," he says. "So for this business, I created the most elaborate spreadsheets and models you've ever seen. And I was wrong about everything." At the time, Garrison's father-in-law dubbed the venture "The Bad Idea Sub Shop".

Unforeseen expenses on building repairs and higher-than-expected food costs ate into the Garrisons' staffing budget. "We didn't start with the number of employees we wanted. We started with the number we could afford," says Charles. The Bad Donkey opened in January 2004 with a lean, five-person team.

Early on, Garrison thought he could avoid the turnover so common in the restaurant industry by hiring full-time employees. However, it took time to find the hiring sweet spot. "After about two years, we finally found the right type to work for us," he says. "It's a part-time high-school junior or senior who can handle some responsibility, comes to work when they're scheduled and, most important, can make our customers smile."

Now that he's discovered a successful candidate profile, Garrison says he doesn't have to place help-wanted ads anymore. "We've got a terrific group of kids who know what we're all about, and they know who would be a good fit to work here," he explains. "It's rare that we hire someone who isn't referred to us by a current employee."

How important are the employees at The Bad Donkey? So important that Garrison refers to his menu of catchy-named items—The Perturbed Bird Sub, The Fancy Schmancy Veggie Pizza, or The Donkeypasto Salad—as a minor detail. "We want The Bad Donkey to be a fun place to eat. And I believe we accomplish that thanks to our employees, whose job it is to make the entire experience a good one for our customers."

The Bad Donkey has grown in just about every measure. Garrison hired an operations manager with solid restaurant experience to help take the business to another level. He's more than doubled the size of the restaurant and added a small ice cream shop off the dining room. Its name? The Dinky Donkey.

Today, Garrison employs, on average, about 30 part-time employees, who usually work three four-hour shifts per week. He credits the hiring of good, motivated employees and the know-how of an experienced operations manager for giving him the confidence to consider expanding to new locations.

Sounds like The Bad Donkey wasn't such a bad idea after all.

sample document: **Employment Application Form**

Employment Application

Application Date _____
Position Applied For _____
How did you find out about this position ? _____

PERSONAL INFORMATION
Name _____
Address _____
City, State, Zip Code _____
Phone Number _____
Email Address _____
Social Security Number _____
If you are under age 18, please provide your date of birth ____/____/____
Are you eligible to work in the United States? Yes _____ No _____

AVAILABILITY
Days and Hours Available
Monday ____ Tuesday ____ Wednesday ____ Thursday ____ Friday ____ Saturday ____ Sunday ____
What date are you available to start work? ____/____/____

EDUCATION
High School
School name _____
Location _____ I f not, did you receive your GED? Yes _____ No _____
Did you graduate? Yes _____ No _____

Colleges Attended
Please list each college you attended and all degrees, undergraduate or graduate, you earned
College name _____
Location _____
Dates attended: From _____ To _____ Field of study _____
Number of years attended _____
Degrees earned _____

College name _____
Location _____
Dates attended: From _____ To _____ Field of study _____
Number of years attended _____
Degrees earned _____

ADDITIONAL QUALIFICATIONS
Please list any licenses, special skills, training, or awards that are relevant to the job position:
_____
_____

EMPLOYMENT HISTORY

Please list your most recent employment first.

From _____ **To** _____
Employer_____
Address _____
Supervisor_____
Job Title_____Phone_____Email _____
Responsibilities_____
Promotions _____
Salary _____Reason for Leaving _____

From _____ **To** _____
Employer_____
Address _____
Supervisor_____
Job Title_____Phone_____Email _____
Responsibilities_____
Promotions _____
Salary _____Reason for Leaving _____

May We Contact Your Present Employer? Yes _____ No _____

PERSONAL REFERENCES

Please list two references other than relatives or previous employers.

Name _____
Address _____
Phone _____
Relationship _____

Name _____
Address _____
Phone _____
Relationship _____

I understand that if I am hired, my employment is considered "at will," meaning that either the company or I may terminate this employment relationship at any time with or without notice. I certify that information contained in this application is true and complete.

Applicant's Signature _____

chapter 10

Interviewing

" The best executive is the one who has sense enough to pick good men to do what he wants done, and self-restraint to keep from meddling with them while they do it. "
—THEODORE ROOSEVELT

Job interviews are tough. They're nerve-wracking when you're the one being interviewed for a job you really want. But, they can also be surprisingly intimidating when you're on the other side of the desk, doing the hiring. What questions should you ask? What will you say about your company? How will you know who's right for the job? How do you discuss salary?

Most small business owners are new to the hiring process. But even if you've conducted dozens of interviews as part of a previous corporate life, hiring feels decidedly different when the sole responsibility for making a good choice lies with you. However, with the right preparation, that responsibility can be empowering—you get to find and select the best talent to take your business to the next level.

To succeed in the interviewing process, a carefully planned approach—from reviewing resumes to extending a formal offer—makes all the difference. If you do it right, you'll find just the right person or people to add to your team. You won't have to do everything alone.

Review Resumes for Winners

With the word out about your job, ideally you'll attract lots of applicants. How will you go through the inbox of resumes or stack of applications to find just the right candidate?

When the resumes start coming in, keep your job description handy. Look for candidates that clearly meet your requirements. Don't simply be swayed by the fact that an applicant went to your college or engages in your favorite sport. So evaluate applicants by:

■ Their resume or application: how well their background meets your requirements

■ Their cover letter, email or other communication: what it tells you about how professional they are in their approach, their fit and enthusiasm for the job, other impressions you have of them

■ Any other indicators that make them a likely candidate

Fortunately for you—and unfortunately for applicants—some will disqualify themselves by submitting a resume riddled with typos or failing to follow the directions stated in the ad, such as calling despite your "no phone calls" request or failing to include references as indicated. Others will disqualify themselves from consideration by not meeting your stated education or experience requirements.

One process for reviewing resumes is to "grade" each resume as you review them—making a pile of those that get "A's," "B's" and so forth. Plan on calling applicants whose resumes earn an "A" or "B+" for a phone screening interview.

Consider the following questions as you evaluate/grade your candidates:

1. Does their past experience and stated career goal match the opportunity?

2. Has their education or training helped prepare them for this job?

3. Do they have a history of commitment and stability, staying with one employer for a length of time?

4. Does the job history demonstrate advancement and increasing responsibility?

5. Does their resume list any successes or results they've achieved in past jobs, such as sales made, money saved or efficiencies gained?

6. Can they point to specific accomplishments or recognition?

7. Have they worked for a small company before? Do they indicate a specific interest in your business or a small company?

If you're filling an entry-level job and are hiring young people or those just out of school, you can't expect relevant job experience or a long job history. Instead, look for any signs that the applicant is a responsible, capable individual. Look for things such as summer jobs, volunteer work, degrees earned when judging their background.

Not enough applicants? What happens if after you've run your help wanted ad and spread the word, you don't seem to attract any qualified applicants? If very few people responded to your ad and those who did weren't appropriate? You need to review your ad, your expectations and your recruitment campaign. Did your ad make the job seem unattractive? Did you include a salary level too low for prevailing wages? Are you unrealistic in what you're looking for?

If you're certain you're being realistic in your ad, did you put it in the right places? Advertise it enough?

*HIRE*Learning

When to Tell Someone 'No'

Job hunters are nervous. They're anxious to find out if they've made the cut to be considered for a job. You don't want to turn away any potentially qualified candidates too soon—there may be a gem in your "B" pile. But it's polite to let people know once they're definitely no longer in consideration. Most companies wait until they hire someone before sending out any 'rejection' emails/letters. On the other hand, once it's absolutely clear that you will not interview someone or take the interview process any farther, you may want to let them know. How can you do this politely? Send an email or letter. Keep it simple, saying something such as "Thank you for applying for the position. There were many qualified candidates, and the decision was difficult. We hope you'll keep us in mind if we have any future job openings. Good luck in your job search." That way, they can get on with their lives.

Tips to Spot Good & Bad Resumes

GOOD SIGNS IN A RESUME	WARNING SIGNS IN A RESUME
Past on-the-job experience that meets your needs	Little or no past job experience (unless entry level job)
Completed education or training, especially if related to your job needs	Failure to complete degrees, education or schooling
History of continually increasing job responsibilities and titles	History showing lack of promotions or progressing job improvements
Stable employment history; continually employed; stays at jobs for reasonable period of time	History of moving from job to job quickly; gaps in employment history
Personalized cover letter or email showing they've read job description; detailing how they meet your needs	No cover letter or 'blanket' response, indicating little knowledge of your job needs
Any special skills, experience, accomplishments that make them unique	Typos, general sloppiness in resume, cover letter, application

Then you need to run your ad again, but spread your net wider. Advertise again but put your ad in more places, on more online sites and publications. Finally, as you review resumes, are you being overly critical? Are you looking for the absolutely, positively perfect person before you'll even bring them in for an interview? That's not a realistic approach. No one will ever meet all your qualifications and requirements. Select those closest to your ideal, and interview some of them.

Effective Phone Screening

Before scheduling in-person interviews—which can take up a great deal of your time—plan on screening your top potential candidates on the phone. A 15-30 minute phone call can save hours of your time. As you review resumes, you'll find you have some basic questions you'll want answered, such as how much responsibility a candidate really had in a job, what their job duties were, or why there's a year unaccounted for in their job history. A phone screening enables you to find out the answers to these relatively easy questions and decide if you want to bring the candidate in to meet you in-person. The phone screen helps in other ways, too. If you're hiring someone to answer your business' phones, the initial interview gives you a glimpse into how the person interacts on the phone and how they might ultimately represent your company's image when customers call.

Schedule a phone interview just as you would an in-person interview. It's not fair to just call a candidate and catch them off guard. Instead, email or call them to set up a time when you can ask them a few questions. Let them know you're calling in response to a resume they submitted—be specific about the position and your company name to help them identify you. Tell them that, based on their resume, you'd like to schedule a 30-minute phone interview to further explore the opportunity. Explain that your phone-screening process will help you develop a short list of candidates for in-person interviews.

What to have handy for your phone interviews:

- [ ] The job description
- [ ] The candidate's resume
- [ ] Other information they provided (cover letter, work samples, etc.)
- [ ] Your list of questions with room for notes
- [ ] Your calendar, so you can schedule an in-person interview if desired

worksheet: **Phone-Interview Questionnaire/Notes**

Use this worksheet to track the answers to the questions you'll ask job candidates in initial phone interviews.

Candidate Name _____

Phone Interview Date and Time _____

How did you hear about this position? _____

What interests you about it? _____

Why are you looking for a job now? _____

_____

Tell me a bit more about the work experience listed on your application. _____

Describe the experience you had with (specific equipment, software, etc.).

_____

Tell me about the experience you've had working directly with customers/clients (if applicable)?

_____

Why do you think you're a good candidate for this job? _____

_____

What kinds of education or special training have you had that will help you succeed in this position?

_____

What are you looking for in your next job? _____

_____

What salary (or hourly rate) are you looking for? _____

Are you willing to have a drug test/credit check/background check (as appropriate and applicable)? _____

_____

Other questions _____

_____

Schedule in-person interview? _____

If appropriate, let them know where—such as your website—they can review more information about your company before the call.

Think of the phone screening as a mini-interview. Your goal is to determine if the applicant is someone you want to interview in person. Be prepared with a list of questions that expand on what you learned by reviewing resumes. Some questions you can ask include:

- How did you hear about this position?

- What about this job interested you?

- Why are you looking for a job now?

- Can you tell me more about your recent jobs?

- Why do you think you're a good candidate for this job?

- How much experience do you have working with (specific equipment, software, etc.)?

- Do you have experience in dealing directly with customers/clients?

- What are your salary requirements?

- Are you willing to undergo credit/drug/background checks? (if applicable)

Add specific questions as they relate to the duties of your particular job. If, for instance, this is a sales position, ask about their experience in sales—how much they sold in a year, how that compared to the sales in previous years, how it compared to other salespeople in the same company.

As always in every interview with a job prospect: Listen more than you talk. Don't monopolize the conversation. Always ask: Do you have any questions for me?

Take notes while conducting your phone interviews. Later, you may not remember which candidate said what, and you'll want to refer to your notes when you bring candidates in for a face-to-face interview. If a candidate says something notable on the phone, ask them to expand on it in person.

In your phone call screening, always let candidates know what to expect. For those that you know you want to meet in person, schedule an appointment. For others, tell them you're considering many qualified applicants and you'll get back to them if you want to schedule an in-person interview.

In-Person Interviews That Click

You've compiled your list of job responsibilities and essential qualifications, reviewed the resumes, and conducted phone screening interviews to narrow down the field to the most promising candidates. Now, with your whittled-down list of applicants in hand, you're ready to conduct in-person interviews with your top candidates.

Preparing for the Interviews

As a small business—especially if this is your first employee—you don't have an "H.R." or Human Relations department to conduct interviews for you. There's no one else to put in charge of figuring out who to hire. As the business owner, you're the one who has to figure out exactly how to conduct the interview—including the logistics. After all, you may not even have a place of business yet or you work out of your home. Where and when will you hold your interviews? And who will participate?

- **Where.** Your place of business, if you have one, is the natural place to conduct interviews, as long as you have a quiet, private place to do so. If, for example, you work out of an office, interview your candidates there. If you have a shop, restaurant, manufacturing plant or other somewhat public location, hold interviews in your office, any other private space, or find a time when others won't be present. It is generally not fair to ask a candidate to answer questions when others can easily overhear.

  If you work out of your home, haven't secured your workspace or business location yet, or don't have a private place to conduct an interview, try to find another reasonably private place to hold the meeting. If you have access to a colleague or friend's office, that's a good choice. But even a local coffee shop or café can work. If you need to hire a lot of people at one time (perhaps for your new restaurant, or recently-funded company), you may want to search for local or campus job fairs where you can interview a number of candidates at once.

If this is an important hire—especially if it's your very first employee—and you will work closely with the person, perhaps even in close quarters (including your home), you may want to schedule a second interview with your top prospect. It's often a good idea to do this second interview over lunch at a restaurant. This type of setting encourages a candidate to 'let their hair down,' and you'll get a better sense of a person in this more comfortable environment.

■ **When.** It's often a good idea to schedule a number of interviews for one morning or afternoon, so you can block off that time on your appointment book. Schedule every job interview at a time when you won't be interrupted. It's not fair—and you won't get a truly good impression of a candidate—if business calls or questions constantly disturb you. No matter when you decide to conduct the interview, you should be there before the candidate is scheduled to arrive, to find out how punctual (or not) a person is.

■ **Who.** Of course, you will conduct the interview with each applicant—after all, it's your business, and you have to decide if the candidate is a good fit for you. But are there others that the candidate will be working for or with? For example, if you run a retail business, will a shift manager supervise the candidate? Or do you have an office manager who'll supervise the administrative assistant or shipping clerk? You'll probably want to bring them in to the interview process at some point. You may want them in on the entire interview, bring them in for the second half of an interview, or schedule a second interview with them for the candidates you like the most.

Even if you work entirely alone, there may be others whose opinion you'd trust to participate in the selection process. Perhaps you want a trusted advisor, like an accountant, attorney, or business colleague to talk with the candidates, especially if the position is an important one in your company. This is less appropriate for the first round of interviews, but you could bring them in for a second, follow-up interview with one or two finalists.

Ten Hiring Do's and Don'ts

1. Do pre-screen candidates on the phone before an in-person interview.

2. Do interview several candidates—at least three if at all possible.

3. Do listen more than you talk.

4. Do be realistic—about job responsibilities, experience required, salary and benefits.

5. Do stick to the same evaluation process for each candidate.

6. Do prepare candidates for the interview. Do you want to see samples of their work? Will you test them? Let them know ahead of time.

7. Don't make promises of job security.

8. Don't hire someone just because you know them.

9. Don't be overly impressed by credentials from big corporations or advanced degrees from well-known universities.

10. Don't be swayed by your first impression. Let the conversation flow for awhile. For important jobs, arrange for a second in-person interview with your top prospect.

SUCCESS STORY

Cultural Fit Comes First at Growing Tech Company

Like so many innovations, Meebo developed from necessity and creativity—and a bit of frustration. Seth Sternberg, Sandy Jen and Elaine Wherry had wanted to work together for years. While working at Wherry's apartment one day, Jen, who relied heavily on instant messaging to communicate with colleagues and friends, couldn't access her IM accounts. The idea behind Meebo was born: a web-based IM service that could integrate a bunch of IM accounts: AOL, Yahoo, MSN, Google and other instant-messaging platforms. "I was still in business school and both Sandy and Elaine had full-time jobs, but we worked nights and weekends to get the business off the ground," Sternberg says. In 2005, they were able to raise money from blue-chip venture capital firms and launch Meebo.com

Of course, a VC-funded business must have gleaming office space filled with young coders, right? Not this one. When Meebo moved from Wherry's apartment into an office, the staff consisted of just the three partners. "Our plan was to keep the business small until the scale of Meebo got out of whack," says Sternberg. The company remained lean even as its users grew. Rather than roll out a series of new features, Jen concentrated on keeping the servers running while Wherry cranked out the code that powered Meebo. Soon, though, the popular site reached a tipping point and the time to hire had come. But instead of hiring the employee the team wanted to hire (an operations manager), they filled the role they needed to fill: an office manager to keep the day-to-day details humming along.

The company takes hiring seriously, with a staffing philosophy that focuses first and foremost on a candidate's work style – Will they fit in our fast-paced culture of collaboration and innovation? A review of skill sets comes later. Meebo uses a checklist to gauge how a potential employee might adapt to the company's culture. Then, in addition to personal interviews with the founders and other key leaders, the candidate participates in a work-related simulation—writing a piece of code or making a pitch to an advertiser about Meebo, for example.

Today, with more than forty million users, Meebo employs more than fifty staffers—mostly full-timers as well as a handful of interns. Sternberg admits the company's hiring formula is rigorous, but believes it pays off in the long run. "We've found that hiring actually slows productivity in the short term when you add up training time and assimilation," says Sternberg. "But then you'll see productivity rise and, as you add more staff, productivity gains are realized much sooner."

Looking ahead, the company plans to stick with Sternberg's culture-first hiring mantra that has served it so well: "The team is more important than the idea."

Interview Tips & Techniques

With every step of the interview process, preparation is key. Here are some interview best practices to consider when planning how you'll spend your face-to-face time:

- **Plan your questions ahead of time.** Don't wait until a job applicant is sitting in front of you to figure out what to ask. Take time well before the first interview to make a list of things you'd like to know about them, and think of probing questions to ask. Think back to the phone interview. Did anything jump out at you that you'd like to explore further?

- **Ask open-ended questions.** When crafting your questions, avoid those that can be answered with a simple yes or no. Also avoid leading questions with an obvious right answer. You want open-ended, thought provoking questions that begin with *what, when, where, how* or *why.* Those questions require the candidate to relay more information and provide insight into who they are.

- **Set the tone.** Start with a firm handshake and a friendly smile. Polite, just-getting-to-know you chatter for the first couple of minutes can break the ice and put everyone at ease.

- **Tell the candidate what to expect.** Explain the process and expected length of the interview—then stick to it. Let them know that you'll take notes during the interview (jot down what they say, not your opinions, at this stage).

- **Plan what you'll say about your company.** The best candidates may have more than one job interview, so you want to tell potential candidates not just about the job they'll be doing, but about the upside of working at your company. Whatever gets you excited—your mission statement, why you started your business, your 5-year plan—share it. Be positive but be honest.

- **Review your benefits.** Take some time to discuss your benefits plan. Many applicants are particularly motivated by benefits, especially health insurance. If you offer these benefits, make sure applicants know. You don't need to go into any depth, just share what you will offer. Also, if you have any creative benefits or perks, be sure to include those to make your business even more attractive to job seekers.

- **Don't make promises you can't keep.** Never make any promises about job security, salary increases, or career advancement. Those can get you in legal trouble later.

- **Remember to listen.** During interviews, don't do all the talking. It's appropriate to explain the job, and in many cases, to sell the job to the candidate, but most of the time the candidate should be talking, not you.

- **Know what you can't ask.** Be careful! Some questions are illegal. You can't, for example, ask whether a candidate is planning on having a child, their marital status, religion, or age. But it's perfectly legal to ask about hobbies, interests, and long-term goals.

- **Put them to the test.** Get a feel for "hands-on" ability by asking candidates to apply their knowledge to a realistic scenario. Ask a potential office manager how they would improve a particular process. Have a candidate for a marketing position suggest improvements to a page on your Web site or to some of your marketing materials.

- **Leave time for questions.** At the end of the interview, always ask if the applicant has any questions for you. See how they think and find out what's important to them. Expect the best candidates to ask you meaningful questions about the job. Questions about your products and services show an interest in how your business operates. It's reasonable that they'll ask about salaries and wages. But if the only questions are about things such as vacation, work hours, and money, then they may not be seriously evaluating whether the duties of the job are a good fit for them. By letting the candidate ask some of the final questions, you can get insights that lead you closer to hiring your first employee.

Questions You Legally Can and Can't Ask a Job Candidate

NO	YES
What is your maiden name? Do you go by Ms. or Mrs.?	What is your name?
What is your date of birth? How old are you?	Are you over the age of 18?
When did you graduate from high school? College?	Did you graduate from high school? College?
Are you an American citizen? Where were you born? What is your nationality?	Are you eligible to work in the United States?
What language did you speak growing up?	Do you speak any languages other than English that could prove useful in this position?
Are you married? Do you plan on having children? Do you have children? Have you arranged for childcare?	Do you have any conflicts with the company work schedule?
Which religious holidays do you observe?	Can you work on holidays and weekends?
Do you have a disability? Do you suffer from any chronic illnesses? Do you take any prescription medications?	Can you perform (physical tasks relevant to the job description) with reasonable accommodation to any of your particular needs?
Have you ever been arrested?	Have you ever been convicted of a felony?
Are you a member of the Army Reserve?	Do you have military experience?

Remember, the interview process is a two-way street. Your top candidates will also be deciding whether they want to work for you. How will you make an impression? For one, relax and be yourself. You'll get the best feel for who's really right for the job that way—and candidates will get the most accurate understanding of what it would be like to work for you.

Interview Questions—What to Ask

Choose a certain set of questions that you'll ask each interviewee. That way, you'll have a solid basis for comparison at the end. Also leave time for discussion tailored to the applicant's experience.

Self-Appraisal Questions. Find out how candidates perceive themselves by asking how they would describe their ability to complete specific tasks. To find out even more, ask the candidate about someone else's opinion, such as "What would your previous manager say about how you…?"

Situation-Based Questions. Think of a real-world situation that your new employee will be in, then ask a "what-if" question about it. You want to know how they would apply past experience in their new job.

Strength and Weaknesses Questions. Ask your candidate directly what they think their strengths and weaknesses are. Follow up with questions on how they developed that strength, or how they plan to overcome their weakness.

11 questions to ask your candidates

1. Why do you want this position?

2. What strengths do you rely on in your current job to be successful?

3. What tools and techniques do you use to stay organized?

4. Can you share an instance when you had to make a decision and your manager was unavailable?

5. Suppose you are in a situation where deadlines and changes are coming fast and furious. How would you handle it?

6. Do you have an example of a time when you delivered exceptional customer or client service?

7. What kind of additional training do you think you'd benefit from?

8. Tell me about a time that you received constructive feedback at work. How did you respond? How did you implement the feedback?

9. Can you tell me about a time when you suggested a better way to perform a process at work?

10. Tell me about a goal that you have achieved—in your personal life or at work—and why it was important to you.

11. Where do you see yourself in five years?

Red flags: when to proceed with caution

Watch for these tell-tale signs that something is amiss when you meet your job candidate in person:

- They arrive late

- They're dressed sloppily or inappropriately for a job interview

- They smoke, chew gum, take calls or text during the interview

- They never make eye contact with you

- They have no questions about the company, job duties or other relevant questions (unless they just appear shy)

- They have trouble communicating with you. If you find yourself thinking, "Maybe I just didn't ask the questions very well," consider it a sign that you'd likely have ongoing communication issues.

Make a note of any of these 'red flags' so you'll remember these issues when you evaluate your finalists and make a decision on who you want to hire to help you grow your company. That's the next step in your hiring process.

Close Strong: How to End the Interview

WHAT TO DO	WHAT TO SAY
Find out if the candidate has anything to add or any questions.	Is there anything you want to tell me that we haven't had the opportunity to talk about? Do you have any questions for me?
Promote your company again.	As a unique small business that offers (what appeals to candidates), I hope you can understand why I'm excited to grow the business. We offer health, dental and vision benefits and a 401K.
Invite the candidate to contact you with questions that come up.	Here's my card. Just send an email if you think of anything else you'd like to tell or ask me.
Let the candidate know how and when they can expect to hear from you.	I am interviewing for the remainder of the week and plan to make a final decision by (date). I will call you.
Thank them for their time.	Thank you for taking the time to meet with me today and for telling me more about your experience. Let me walk you out.

Making the Offer and Negotiating

> *There is something that is much more scarce, something rarer than ability. It is the ability to recognize ability.*
>
> —ROBERT HALF

If you're fortunate, you'll have several candidates for your job opening. How will you choose among them? Or, perhaps you'll have one candidate that is clearly the front-runner who you're excited about getting on your team. You'll still want to check them out to make certain your impression of them squares with their background.

If you're a bit less fortunate, you may have one or two "maybes"—candidates who appear to be qualified but you're not entirely 100% confident of. Perhaps you're being unrealistic in your expectations? A good evaluation process and some reference checks can help you clarify your thinking.

Once you've met the candidates and narrowed down the field to one or two strong ones, you need to act quickly. The best candidates may not be available long—even in a tight job market. And if you take too long to decide, they may lose their enthusiasm about working for you even if they're still available.

But—if you truly haven't found anyone who clicks—someone with the experience, attitudes,

background, and personality—then you may need to start the process again, spreading a wider net to attract additional job applicants.

Give yourself time: it's better to leave the job open than to hire the wrong person. In every business, but especially in a small business, each employee has an impact on the success of a company. You want to find the right people to be part of your team.

Once again, making the decision and making the job offer are a process composed of the following steps:

1. Decide on top candidate(s)

2. Perform reference checks

3. Call employee and make offer

4. Get employee's signature for drug and background screening, if necessary

5. Conduct background screens, if necessary

6. Send a formal offer letter

HIRELearning

Small Business Hiring

Working for a small business differs from working for a huge corporation. In a large company, employees typically have clearly defined duties. But your employees—especially your first employees—will likely juggle many tasks and responsibilities, often simultaneously. You need them to use their judgment to make decisions. So search for flexible, smart, independent candidates, preferably with experience working in more small-scale businesses, and who are likely to thrive in a more 'family' environment.

Evaluate Your Candidates

After you've conducted your in-person interviews, you may have to decide between two or more talented people. This is always tough, but it's particularly hard for entrepreneurs hiring for the first time.

As you try to decide how to break a tie between candidates, use an evaluation process to assess the strengths and weaknesses of each candidate. Remember, however, that you'll likely find yourself comparing people with different skills and experiences—one might have more real-life experience, one more education suited for the position, or one might have better references.

Here is one critical thing to keep in mind:

Hire for attitude, train for skills. When advertising for a job, the emphasis is usually on the specific skill set you need—knowledge of computer programs, experience with sales, or the like. But once someone starts the job, their attitude toward work, their enthusiasm for the job, and their willingness to take responsibility makes a major difference in whether they are a great contributor or someone who just plods along. Of course, you need certain skills for some jobs—you're not going to teach someone complex computer programming skills, for example—but when deciding between two fairly equal candidates—especially if the specific skills can be taught easily—your decision should favor the candidate who appears to have the best work attitude.

An evaluation form helps give you a structure for assessing the strengths and weaknesses—and your overall impressions—of the candidates. It's a good idea to fill in an evaluation form as soon as you've met each candidate face-to-face. If you interview multiple candidates across several busy work days, filling out evaluation forms on each one helps prevent "who said what" and "which one was she" questions later.

Going through an evaluation form process helps you in another way as well: it points out the areas where you might need to do some extra training with your successful hire. Let's say you rate your candidate low on having a good phone manner, but they're well-organized and will make a great administrative assistant. If you hire them, you may want to spend extra time training them to improve their telephone skills.

Use an evaluation form, like the one included on the following page, to help crystallize your thoughts.

Challenge your Comfort Zone

People tend to hire people who are similar to themselves. After all, your comfort level is naturally high with those who resemble you. But that means you may not give adequate consideration to those who are less similar to you. So check yourself: are you fairly and honestly evaluating candidates who differ from you in background, age, race, gender, national origin? The best businesses use the talents of diverse people with diverse personalities. They bring fresh perspectives—and possibly help you reach other types of customers as well.

worksheet: Candidate Evaluation Form

NAME:_____   DATE:_____

Check the appropriate box and add additional criteria on which you'd like to evaluate your candidates. Add a row for each requirement. Use the same form for each of your top candidates.

QUALIFICATIONS	GREAT	GOOD	FAIR/ POOR	COMMENTS/DETAILS
Education				
Special training				
Nature of past work experience				
Length of past work experience				
Specific skill:				
Specific skill:				
Specific skill:				
Other relevant background				
Grasp of job duties				
Realistic self appraisal				
Appropriate career goals				
Interested in field or company				
Attitude, enthusiasm				
Communication skills				
Achievement oriented				
Other				
OVERALL EVALUATION				

Additional Comments:

Check References & Backgrounds

Once you've selected your candidate, you'll be eager to get them started. But hold on! First, take the time to check the references of your top candidates. Reference checks verify claims made by the candidates and provide valuable outside perspective on your future employee. Even if you have no reason to doubt the honesty of an applicant, you can learn a lot from conducting reference checks.

Check references near the end of the interviewing process, when you are close to making a decision. Whose references do you check? Your top candidate, of course. But if you're deciding between two candidates, reference checks may help make your decision easier. You can legally conduct reference checks on more than one candidate. That is not true for all types of background checks (see below). Be sure to obtain permission from the candidates before you check their references—you don't want to get them in trouble with their current boss.

Always make a reference check on the phone—not just via email. You'll get more information and more insight when you talk with an individual. Who should you call? Immediate and past supervisors give you the most relevant information about how a candidate performed on the job. In addition to supervisors, ask to speak with others who could have observed or interacted with the candidate in a work setting. Barring work-related references, ask for school or volunteer work references. If you have to rely on personal references, ask more probing questions about the candidate that will give you some idea of their likely work attitudes.

When you make the call, introduce yourself and ask for fifteen minutes to discuss the qualifications of the person under consideration. After a brief description of the job, ask specific questions—but once again, try to be open-ended to get as much information as possible—such as:

- What were the candidate's primary job duties?

- How would you describe the candidate's job performance?

- What duties did the candidate particularly enjoy or do well?

- What value did the candidate add to your company?

- What did fellow employees like best about the candidate?

- What job duties required you to give more direction than others?

- What types of jobs do you think this candidate would excel in?

- Are there any jobs that would be inappropriate for the candidate?

- What kind of skills or training would you suggest to make the applicant an even better employee?

- Can you tell me a bit about the candidate's attendance—were they prompt, frequently absent?

- Why did the candidate leave?

- Would you rehire this candidate?

Background checks

Once you've decided on someone for the job and offered them the position—and only after they've been selected—for some jobs, you may want to—or need to—conduct a more thorough background investigation. Many large corporations routinely check all new employees' histories. That's not necessary—and it can be quite expensive—for most small businesses. But there are many instances when you'll want to do a background check: if your employee is going to have access to your finances, will be driving, needs professional licenses or certification, or is required to be bonded.

Before you can conduct most of these checks, legally, you must have already selected the candidate for the job and offered them the position. On top of that, you need the candidate's written permission. It is a good idea to get that any time you dig into a candidate's history. You certainly need their permission to do a credit check, check their driving record, or conduct a drug test.

Turn to a professional background screening company to administer these tests for you. There are many companies that provide these services to employers. Avoid online companies that advertise instant checks. Instead, choose a reputable, established company such as Sterling (www.sterlingtesting.com), Intellicorp (www.intellicorp.net), or Kroll (www.krollbackgroundscreening.com). Screening and testing fees add up, so limit yourself to background checks that directly relate to your business. If you run a limousine service, obtain a copy of your candidate's driving record. If you own a hair salon, you won't need to visit the DMV, but you will want to verify that you new stylist has a license. If a candidate will have access to money, you may want to do a credit check.

Making the Offer

Congratulations! You've selected your first employee. That's a big step for both of you. Now, you need to formally offer them the job and get their acceptance. If you need to do some types of background checks (such as drug tests or credit checks), you'll need to get their written permission.

Tailor Your Background Checks

TYPE OF JOB	TYPE OF SCREENING	REQUIRES EMPLOYEE CONSENT?	HOW DO I CONDUCT THIS CHECK?
Work with children, elderly, enter customers' homes	Criminal history, Credit report	Yes	Third-party service
Handle money, have access to financial information	Credit report, Criminal history	Yes	Order a credit report from TransUnion.com, Experian.com or Equifax.com. If you decide not to hire based on a bad credit report, you must give a copy of the report to the job candidate. Third-party service
Drive company or personal vehicles or operate machinery	Driving record, possibly drug test	Yes	Department of Motor Vehicles Third-party service
Require a professional license or certification	Professional license and certification validation	No	Appropriate licensing agency. Ask if the agency has ever disciplined your candidate.
Require a degree or diploma for the position?	Education verification	Yes	Applicant's former school(s)

sample document: Offer Letter

[Date]

Dear_____,

On behalf of XYZ Marketing, Inc., I'm pleased to offer you a position as Office Coordinator. In this role, your salary will be _____ per pay period, which is equivalent to a rate of _____ per year. You will report directly to me. Your first day of work will be _____. Work hours are from 8:30 am to 5 pm.

The offer described above is contingent upon the results of your reference check, background check, and credit check. Please sign and return an authorization to conduct a credit check that accompanies this letter.

A summary of your benefits is enclosed with this letter. If you have any questions, please don't hesitate to contact me.

On your first day, you will be asked to complete a Form I-9 in compliance with the Immigration Reform and Control Act. As part of this compliance, you must present us with documents that identify you and indicate you are eligible to work in the United States. This must be done within three days of hire.

You will need to complete and submit the benefits enrollment forms within 30 days of your date of hire. If you have any questions regarding the I-9 or benefits information, please contact me and I'll be happy to walk you through the process.

I look forward to working with you and to the contributions you will make to XYZ Marketing, as well as the opportunity to provide you with professional growth. Please indicate your acceptance of our offer by signing below and returning one copy of the letter, with your original signature, to me no later than [date].

Sincerely,

[Your name and signature]

I accept/decline (please circle one) XYZ Marketing's offer of employment. I understand that my employment with XYZ Marketing, Inc. is considered "at will," meaning that either the company or I may terminate this employment relationship at any time without cause or notice.

_____

[Employee name and signature]

So how do you go about actually getting your selection on board?

1. **Make the call.** Once you've selected your candidate, place a phone call to them as soon as you can. You don't want to lose them or make them feel discouraged. If they accept the offer, they'll want to know when you want them to start work. You may want them tomorrow, but if they're currently employed, allow them a reasonable time to provide notice to their current employer. Even those who are out-of-work may have some personal things they need to take care of. Expect a minimum of two weeks before a successful candidate can start.

   In your call, be certain to let them know how excited you are to have them join your company. Set a starting date and time. Ask them if they need or want any information before their first day. They may need to know about parking or public transportation. Let them know you will send them a formal offer letter.

2. **Send an offer letter.** It's a good idea to get in the practice of giving each new hire a formal offer letter. Although you can send this via email, you want them to counter-sign the letter showing that they understand and agree to the terms. Your offer letter includes your official offer of employment, details of the salary or hourly wage you're offering, the date of employment, benefits, and other pertinent information, such as work hours.

3. **Request consent for background checks.** If appropriate, explain that the offer of employment is contingent on any pre-employment screening you wish to do—drug screen, credit check, background check, etc. Most importantly, the letter indicates that you are hiring the employee on an "at will" basis—meaning you can terminate them at any time for any or no reason.

Use the sample letter in this chapter to develop your formal job offer. Include with the offer letter the consent forms relevant to the background checks you plan on running, if any. You can use the sample authorization forms included in this chapter as a starting point.

Negotiating

What if the only thing that stands between you and the candidate of your dreams is the salary range? How much can you negotiate on salary or wages? How much should you? And how do you negotiate effectively?

Many—if not most—job applicants may try to negotiate. After all, they're going to test the waters to see if they can possibly make more money, especially if you've waited until they're the final candidate (and they know it) before you bring up the subject of salary. If you've already discussed salary during the in-person interview, they may be reluctant to bring up the issue again, or they may ask about raises.

If your salary or wages are considerably lower than other prevailing wages, expect every qualified candidate to negotiate, and if you want good people, you'll have to change your pay scale.

As you begin to negotiate, first, you have to understand your budgetary limitations. Unless you are hiring for a position that will bring in more cash—such as an outside sales person you can't count on more money coming in as a direct result of this hire. Ideally, because you've hired someone, your business will grow. For instance, hiring an assistant will free you of administrative tasks so you can go out and make more money doing what you can charge clients for. But this is not certain, so you have to be realistic about your cash flow. Remember, you'll pay your employee before you pay yourself (legally, you have to pay them; you can skip your own paycheck without government interference). So, the first and foremost consideration is: Can you really afford more money?

Next, how valuable—and exceptional—is the candidate? If, in fact, this really is the candidate of your dreams, you're probably going to want to do

sample document: Drug Screen Authorization Letter

I, [applicant name], do hereby agree to submit to testing to be performed by [laboratory name/address] for detection of drugs and alcohol. I give permission for test results to be released to XYZ Marketing, Inc.

I understand that positive test results, refusal to be tested, or any attempt to affect the test results or test sample will result in withdrawal of my application for employment, withdrawal of any provisional employment offer I have received from XYZ Marketing, Inc., or termination of employment, depending on when results are received.

Applicant Signature_____

Date_____

Witnessed by_____

Date_____

sample document: Credit Report Authorization

Authorization to Obtain a Consumer Credit Report and Release of Information

Pursuant to the federal Fair Credit Reporting Act, I hereby authorize XYZ Marketing, Inc., and its designated agents and representatives to conduct a comprehensive review of my background through a consumer report and/or an investigative consumer report to be generated for employment, promotion, reassignment or retention as an employee. I understand the scope of the consumer report/investigative consumer report may include, but is not limited to, the following areas: verification of Social Security number; current and previous residences; employment history, including all personnel files; education; references; credit history and reports; criminal history, including records from any criminal justice agency in any or all federal, state or county jurisdictions; birth records; motor vehicle records, including traffic citations and registration; and any other public records.

I, _____, authorize the complete release of these records or data pertaining to me which an individual, company, firm, corporation or public agency may have. I understand that I must provide my date of birth to adequately complete said screening and acknowledge that my date of birth will not affect any hiring decisions. I hereby authorize and request any present or former employer, school, police department, financial institution or other persons having personal knowledge of me to furnish XYZ Marketing, Inc., or its designated agents with any and all information in their possession regarding me in connection with an application of employment. I am authorizing that a photocopy of this authorization be accepted with the same authority as the original.

I hereby release XYZ Marketing, Inc., and its agents, officials, representatives or assigned agencies, including officers, employees or related personnel, both individually and collectively, from any and all liability for damages of whatever kind, which may at anytime result to me, my heirs, family or associates because of compliance with this authorization and request to release. You may contact me as indicated below.

I understand that, pursuant to the federal Fair Credit Reporting Act, if any adverse action is to be taken based upon the consumer report, a copy of the report and a summary of the consumer's right will be provided to me.

By signing below, I certify that the above information is true and correct.

Signature _____

Date _____

everything you can to land them. It that means negotiating on salary, you'll need to do so. If you truly believe the candidate will materially improve and grow your company, you need to take that into consideration as you enter the negotiation process. Or, if they have a special skill that's in demand, you'll need to sweeten the deal.

When negotiating on salary or wages, ask the candidate what salary they need to accept the job. Make them give you a specific number—especially as you've already offered a salary to them. Then you can see how far apart you are and whether there's room in the middle you can both live with. Remember, if a candidate is very unhappy about the salary, they are likely to start hunting for another job as soon as they can, and you'll be faced with the entire hiring process again.

Other approaches to consider as part of a negotiating process:

- **Increased benefits.** In any salary negotiation, try to ascertain exactly what the candidate cares about most. Would they be willing to accept some increase in their non-financial benefits—such as increased vacation, more flexible work hours—instead of just cash? These don't cost you anything more out-of-pocket and may enable you to land the candidate even if your cash is really tight.

- **Future raises.** You can also offer the possibility of increased responsibilities and/or pay in the future. If you know you'll be willing to offer a definite increase in a specific period of time ("I can give you a raise from $15 an hour to $20 an hour in six months"), that's often a way to win a candidate. However, recognize that if you state it this way, you will have to actually go ahead and increase the salary whether or not you're happy with their performance. A more satisfactory approach is to state that there may be a raise after a performance review in six months. That way, you have the option of not increasing their wages if their work quality doesn't live up to your expectations.

- **Training or advancement.** Many of the best candidates want to get ahead. One way both of you can benefit is by offering them additional training and the real likelihood of moving up on the job with increasing responsibility and authority. Working for a small business often gives an individual the chance to considerably expand their job skill sets, and this is something they often can't get working for bigger companies. For instance, your administrative assistant might be interested in learning about marketing, how to develop and run a website, or participate in social networking. These skills will make your candidate more marketable for future employment and can make your offer more enticing.

Don't forget to mention any other benefits you offer, especially ones they're unlikely to find with other employers. All of these make your job offer more competitive.

Follow Up!

What happens to those candidates who didn't make the cut? You've got to let them know—gently.

No one enjoys informing a good candidate that the job went to someone else. But it's the polite thing to do, especially after a long interview process. Let the candidate know as soon as you have made your decision, and don't provide a long, detailed explanation. If you've spent a long time with a candidate, you may want to give them a call, but that can be awkward for both of you. Although it seems somewhat brusque, the easiest way to handle this is through a polite rejection letter.

Keep your rejection letter simple and to the point. This extra step may seem like a burden to a busy small business owner making that first hire. But taking the time to inform your anxiously awaiting candidates of your decision will help establish your reputation as a good place to work and do business—it may just lead to additional applicants or clients. By extending this courtesy to your job candidates, you will stand out in the crowd.

sample document: Rejection Letter

[Date]

Name

Address

City, State, Zip

Dear [Name]:

Thank you for taking the time to apply for the position of Office Coordinator at XYZ Marketing. I was fortunate to attract a number of strong candidates such as yourself. I regret to inform you, however, that I have chosen another individual for the position.

I wish you every success with your future job search. Thank you for your interest in the company.

Sincerely,

[Your name, title and signature]

Section Five:
The First Day and Beyond

CHAPTER 12   *Day One: Start off Strong* 156

CHAPTER 13   *Becoming the Boss* 164

Day One:
Start off Strong

"Don't tell people how to do things, tell them what to do and let them surprise you with their results."
—GEORGE S. PATTON

Congratulations—you've hired your first employee! You've scheduled their start date. Before you know it, they'll be arriving for their first day on the job. It's exciting for you to have *finally* found someone, but now you have to get them going so they can help you grow your business.

Welcome Aboard!

First days on the job can be nerve-wracking for both managers and employees. But it doesn't have to be a high-pressure situation for either of you. You can do several things to make the first day a smooth one and get both of you acclimated to your new situation quickly.

1. **Create a detailed schedule for the day.** Nothing—and that's *nothing*—is more disconcerting and uncomfortable for new hires than to show up on the first day only to have nothing to do. So plan ahead. Establish an agenda and allot time for such things as completing legal and benefits paperwork, reviewing companies policies, being

introduced to their immediate tasks as well as longer-term responsibilities and training should begin immediately. Don't forget to schedule such things as time for setting up email or voicemail accounts, or for employees to organize their workspaces. And you should probably schedule a little more time for each item on your agenda than you might otherwise anticipate so you can answer all of their questions (there will probably be many). At the end of the day, do a quick review and make sure they know exactly what they will be doing when they show up for Day Two.

2. **Complete legal paperwork.** The government requires new employees to complete a number of legal documents soon after they're hired, so get this out of the way on day one. You may have some documents you need them to complete for workers' compensation, health care, retirement or other benefits. And it's a good idea to have each employee give you a document with full contact information and emergency numbers. If you know you'll be interrupted by phone calls or

otherwise busy during day one, they can fill this out while they wait for you to be available again.

3. **Find a workspace.** Before your employee shows up for work on day one, figure out where they're going to work. Do you have a separate room or area in your office? If not, you'll have to carve out some space for them to work comfortably and not disturb you. You'll need to equip it with a desk or table. Employees also need some place to store their own belongings—a locker in a restaurant, closet in a store, drawers in a desk. If you're hiring a number of hourly workers, where and how will they sign in and keep track of their hours? Think through these issues before employees show up on day one.

4. **Prepare other tools for the job.** In addition to a desk—or whatever is an appropriate workspace in your office—line up some of the other tools the employee will need to work effectively. Some of these you'll need on day one or soon thereafter; others (such as a company key, cell phone or credit card), you may want to wait a few months to make certain the employee is working out. Another useful tool to consider is capturing all critical phone numbers, email addresses, or access codes your employee will need on day-to-day basis in one document so that they don't have to ask you for this information every time they need it.

Which of these tools you provide depends on the job responsibilities of your employee:

- ☐ Office or work supplies
- ☐ Uniforms or other clothing/accessories
- ☐ Computer with Internet access
- ☐ Email account in their name
- ☐ Business cards
- ☐ Key background materials or customer files
- ☐ Office keys/access codes/security access card
- ☐ Cell phone
- ☐ Business credit card

Start on a Friday?

Is Monday the busiest day of your week? Have your new employee come in on a day when things are much slower. Clear your calendar of meetings and appointments on their first day. They need—and deserve—your attention to help them get started right, and they'll be more productive sooner.

5. **Give them a tour.** Even if you're working out of your home, your new employee needs to get acquainted with the basic layout of their work environment. Where's the bathroom? The coffee pot? Where's nearby parking or transportation? Places to get lunch? Help them become familiar with their new surroundings.

6. **Begin on-the-job training and complete first task(s).** One of the most important things you can do on Day One is to let new hires "get their hands dirty" with their new job responsibilities. The next section of this chapter discusses training in more detail. But on day one, plan to keep the training manageable and don't overwhelm your new hire. Concentrate on one or two tasks that are representative of their responsibilities.

7. **Create a calendar.** Before the employee arrives, pull together a schedule for the employee that shows any key dates or events on the horizon. This can include things such as when certain reports are due to clients, when regular customer meetings or events are scheduled, and even when you plan on being out of the office.

8. **Go out to lunch.** You spent a significant amount of time getting to know your prospective employee during the interview process. However, stakes were so high at that point that the candidate might have been nervous and not able to relax. Now that they're hired, treat them

to lunch and use the time to get to know them better in a more relaxed setting. If you've hired a number of employees at once—for example, if your new store, restaurant or service business is just launching—hold a group lunch so you can begin building a sense of team spirit.

9. **Visit a customer.** Use your employee's first day as an opportunity to introduce them—in person—to a key customer or client. This will serve two purposes. First, the customer will meet a key point person for their future interactions with your business. Second, your new employee will see first-hand how you treat customers.

10. **Inform your customers.** Since you've been solo thus far, you've been the only one your clients or customers talk to on the phone, exchange emails with, meet in the storefront, or otherwise interact with. It's a good idea to prepare them to hear a new "voice" by introducing them to your new employee. Send them a short note or email announcing the hire and explain the employee's new role. If appropriate, be sure to include your employee's name and short bio with yours on your website's "About Us" page.

*HIRE*Learning

Day One Government Documents

Form I-9: All U.S. employers must verify the employment eligibility and identity of all employees hired to work in the U.S. Employees must complete an I-9 form, Employment Eligibility Verification form, and show proof of identity within three business days of the first day of work. Keep this in your records. You do not have to file it with the government.

Form W-4: Employees must also complete a W-4, indicating the number of dependents they're claiming for income tax purposes, so that you can withhold the correct federal income tax from their paychecks. Once again, you keep this in your records; it does not need to be filed with any government agencies.

Find more information on these and other legal documents in Chapter 4 on Employment Law.

sample document: Employee Introduction Email

[Client or customer name]:

I'm delighted to introduce Kristine Anderson as the new member of the XYZ Marketing team. Starting Monday, Kristine will be the voice you hear when you call our office and she will play a significant role in assuring that we meet your needs. She'll be responsible for XYZ's billing, accounting and campaign measurement, and you can call her—as well as me—if you have any questions. Kristine has more than a decade of experience in administration, including working for other marketing and sales organizations. I've been impressed by Kristine's enthusiasm and results-focused approach to her work and know that you will enjoy working with her. If you have any questions, don't hesitate to give me a call. Kristine's new email address is Kristine@xyzmarketing.com.

[Your signature]

worksheet: My Preparation for Day One

GOAL	MANAGEMENT TASK TO COMPLETE IN PREPARATION	√
Provide first-day agenda		
Set my goals—for the first day		
Employment paperwork		
Provide workspace		
Provide equipment (computer, office supplies, etc.)		
Provide other tools, lists, contacts		
Provide calendar, deadlines		
Conduct first day training		
Provide 'operations manual'		
Other:		
Other:		
Other:		
Other:		
Other:		

sample document: Sample Day One Agenda

Welcome, Kristine
Day One Agenda—April 19

9—10 am — Getting Started

Quick tour of office and facilities

Get acquainted with your workspace, computer, set up email and voicemail accounts

Complete required paperwork and forms

10—10:30 am—XYZ Marketing 101

Go over history of company

Review our products and services

Discuss customers, key customers, customer expectations

10:30—noon— Introduction to Job Responsibilities

Review job description

Explain key tasks in greater detail

Review key deadlines, time constraints, expected daily/weekly/monthly deliverables

noon—1 pm: Lunch at Casa Molina

1—4 pm—Day One Training

Review operations manual

Assign first task

Train on how to complete task

Allow time for employee to do task

4—4:30 pm—Customer Phone Call

4:30—5 pm—End of Day Touch Base

What questions can I answer?

What else will help you do the job?

Day One Training

On the first day of work, your employee is going to be eager not only to learn about the business but to get started on the responsibilities they're going to be handling every day and every week. And, of course, you want them to get started too. But you have to be realistic. You want to give them enough information for them to start to do their work, but their head is going to be spinning with so much to take in, so you have to plan your training carefully and keep your expectations appropriate of how much they can learn in just the first day. Remember, training should continue well beyond day one—even beyond week one or the first month. The best businesses train their employees continually.

Your employees need, at minimum, training that delivers the following:

■ Training for their specific tasks

■ Knowledge about your company, product, services

■ Training to increase their broader skills and achieve larger objectives

Keep in mind that by law, you must pay employees during time they spend for training. For instance, they must be paid for days on the job spent in training but also for coming in early, staying late, coming in on a weekend, going to a mandatory class offsite for training, or any other time spent on training.

Training for Specific Job Skills

This type of training represents the most basic, and can encompass everything from helping a new hire understand how to use a computer software program to prepare packages for shipment to answer the phone appropriately.

The first thing to do as you prepare to train your new employee is to refer back to the job description you carefully developed. Think through each of the jobs you've hired them to do, and what they need to do to accomplish each of those tasks.

Some of those tasks must be completed in a precise fashion, such as how to process orders in a merchant account, handle orders for shipping, or enter information into company computer programs. Others may not require absolute precision, but may be tasks you feel strongly about, such as how the phones should be answered or a service provided. For other tasks, your employee can use a great deal of their own judgment or methods to complete. Understanding those differences helps you to better orient and train your new employee.

Take your job description a few steps further by creating an "Operations Manual" or "Job Manual." By writing down the processes and procedures you expect your employee to follow, it becomes a tool for your training, gives you more insight into what you're truly asking your employee to do, and provides them with documentation to refer back to.

Expect to spend considerable time training for specific tasks, whether explaining something as complicated as a company software program or showing exactly how you want a table in your restaurant to be set. How effective and efficient you'll be depends on how complicated the task is, your communication skills, and the learning style of your employees.

As you plan your training, think about training for each task as encompassing three basic steps: tell, show, try.

So for each task you need your employee to learn, go through the following

1. **TELL** them what needs to be done, how it needs to be done precisely, why it needs to be done, and how it relates to the business.

2. **SHOW** them how to do it; have them watch while you do the task, giving them plenty of time for questions.

3. **TRY** have the new employee try to do the task while you watch so that you can give them feedback.

worksheet: **Day One Checklist**

Use this checklist as a guide for covering essential policies, logistics and other items on your employee's first day at work.

EMPLOYEE INFORMATION

Name: _____

Start Date: _____ **Position:** _____

Review Benefits & Policies: Review company policies on the following, how to request vacation, time off, etc.:
- ❑ Vacation
- ❑ Sick leave
- ❑ Holidays
- ❑ Paid time off (PTO)
- ❑ Overtime
- ❑ FMLA/leaves of absence

Review Administrative Procedures:
- ❑ Review job schedule and hours.
- ❑ Review payroll timing, time cards (if applicable), policies and procedures
- ❑ Review policies/best practices of email, telephones, Internet use
- ❑ Review how to handle expense reports, purchase requests, etc.
- ❑ Access to office, keys, security

Facilities
- ❑ Tour of facility
- ❑ Kitchen, coffee, vending machines
- ❑ Parking/transportation
- ❑ Rest rooms
- ❑ Mailbox
- ❑ Copy machine
- ❑ Fax machine
- ❑ Parking/Transportation

Responsibilities & Training
- ❑ Review initial job assignments and training plans
- ❑ Review job description and performance expectations and standards
- ❑ Give employee operations manual
- ❑ Train for specific assignments
- ❑ Discuss future training needs/options

Computers, Equipment: Hardware and software review, including:
- ❑ Company software programs, databases, network
- ❑ Office equipment, including printers, copiers, faxes
- ❑ Cash register, processing orders
- ❑ Any specialized equipment

Training about Your Specific Business

What makes a good salesperson? Someone who really knows and understands the product or service they're selling. It's certainly frustrating, as a customer, to go into a store or restaurant and have the salesperson or waitperson not really know about the products or food. You're likely to buy much less.

Having employees understand your business—your company history, goals, strategy—as well as the products and services you sell helps you succeed. It also helps if they understand a bit about the industry you're in and the competition you face. They can become more productive and motivated employees when they understand the "why" behind the processes and procedures you've implemented.

Employees are more motivated when they feel a sense of purpose for what they do every day. And every business is filling a customer need or meeting a necessary societal goal. You can help your employees stay engaged by sharing what motivates and excites you about your business.

If you want your employees to make suggestions and go the extra mile, make sure they understand the "big picture" strategic goals of your company.

Training to Improve Skills and Capabilities

In addition to training for the specific tasks employees must handle immediately, it's likely that you'll want to help employees improve their capabilities so that they can help you achieve larger job-related objectives and grow your company. The more they learn, the more they can contribute to your company.

This kind of training can be in the "soft skills," such as sales, organization, customer service, presentations, and communication. Or training can be in more specific skills, such as improving their knowledge of software programs.

Generally, this is not necessarily training you'd send employees off to on day one or even week one.

You want to make sure they're a good fit before you invest the time and money for an employee to improve their skill set.

You've got lots of options on how to provide this kind of training. Some include:

- Classes from community colleges, extension courses, universities
- Classes from business training program companies
- Online training courses your employees can do at their desk
- Industry seminars, workshops, conferences
- Local entrepreneurship organization seminars, workshops

When it comes to training, remember one of the best things you can do to make your employees the most productive, and to contribute the most to the success of your business, is to set up your workplace so that they can use their brains and initiative as well as complete jobs in a routine fashion. Of course, for some things, it may be essential that they do things your way. Generally, any task related to finances, sensitive data, or subject to government regulation or laws should follow carefully prescribed processes. This doesn't mean, of course, that you shouldn't be open to suggestions here as well. Your new hire might have experience from a previous job involving, say, credit card processing, that greatly streamlines your existing way of doing things as well as promoting greater security. So listen to their suggestions.

But for many other tasks, you can offer more leeway in how they perform their functions. So give them more than just instructions on how to complete specific tasks: give them your *goals* and *objectives*, making it clear that you respect their input on how best to achieve those goals and objectives. And you must also give them the authority to make some of their own decisions and act on their choices.

When your employees not only perform tasks but think about how best they can do their jobs and grow the company, you all win.

Becoming the Boss

> *"Management is doing things right; leadership is doing the right things."*
> —PETER DRUCKER

This is not a book about leadership or ongoing management of employees—there are plenty of those out there. Still, when you talk about hiring, words like *lead* and *manage* and *motivate* invariably enter the discussion. After all, for the first time you are a bona fide "boss." Whatever your management style—whether you manage by consensus or by making unilateral decisions; whether you have an open-books policy, or keep business matters closer to your chest—you are in fact now in charge. You sign the paychecks. And you must make sure your new hires understand their responsibilities and have been given the training they need to fulfill them to your satisfaction.

In this chapter, you'll learn more about what it's like to wear the boss' hat, what the difference between leading and managing is, and why you need to do both. You'll also spend time exploring how best to motivate and—most importantly—retain employees. After all, you need to ensure that all the hard work you've put into finding, vetting, and bringing

employees on board pays off over the long haul. Then, congratulations! You're on your way to growing your company through hiring—and to making an important contribution to the economy and the business community that will pay off for you emotionally as well as financially.

You're the Boss: Leader or Manager?

What kind of boss do you want to be? The best way to answer this question is to think back on your own experiences as an employee. What leadership and management styles did you respond to? What kind of boss inspired you to produce your best work? Conversely, what sort of management techniques did you find less helpful? Which ones inhibited your creativity or dampened your enthusiasm? The key to determining your own particular style will depend on how you answer questions like these.

What makes a good boss? Many things. But, most bad bosses exhibit some very particular behaviors. You get into trouble as a boss, just as you do as a parent, when you fail to set standards, act fairly, listen, show respect, and offer rewards.

It's important to draw a distinction between being a manager and being a leader. These are two distinctly different roles with two distinctly different skill sets. Optimally, a small business owner or entrepreneur should be able to switch back and forth between the two roles. Practically speaking, such a person is rare. But at the very least you should be conscious of the key attributes of each, and strive to incorporate them into your working style.

First, some basic definitions:

A *leader* is someone who provides guidance and direction—someone who illuminates and shows the way forward toward a goal.

A *manager* is someone who takes a more hands-on and direct approach. To manage implies more direct governance and control than leadership. Rather than focusing on high-level goals, a manager helps people successfully fulfill responsibilities.

Both leaders and managers are necessary to make a business succeed. Yet small businesses usually aren't staffed to have separate people fulfill these roles. So it's often up to you, as the boss, to wear both hats.

And wearing both hats is indeed required. You can't afford to get so wrapped up in managing that you don't lead the company. You'll find your sales pipeline going dry and competitors beating you. On the other hand, putting too much emphasis on leadership can result in problems with day-to-day operations that can hurt your bottom line. If customer service is poor or orders aren't being fulfilled, then you are probably leading too much, and it's time to start managing.

Laying the Groundwork for Good Leadership/Management

Think of the act of transforming yourself into a first-rate boss as a six-step process that involves incorporating aspects of both management and leadership into your style:

1. **Choose a role model.** Most people have a former boss they think of with respect or even fondness. Perhaps this was someone you admired from a distance as having a knack for motivating people to do their very best. Or it might have been a mentor—someone who personally encouraged you, recognized your potential, and opened doors to opportunities. Fix your mind on that person as a role model—someone whose values and work ethic you would like to emulate in your own managerial/leadership style.

Manager vs. Leader—Wearing Both Hats is Required

A MANAGER	A LEADER....
Tells employees what needs to be done	Sets high-level goals and strategy; establishes clear standards and values
Trains employees (or arranges for training) on how to do their jobs well	Keeps the business on track to reach those goals
Monitors/measures success on a daily procedural/process level	Monitors/measures success at the financial/organizational level
Helps prevent things from going wrong	Helps things go right
Fixes problems when they do occur	Empowers others to take action to fix problems

2. **Distill good (and bad) managerial and leadership practices down into a concise list.** Analyze what your chosen role model did—the techniques used to inspire and motivate you. Try to distill them down to *actionable* steps you can take to achieve the same results with your own employees. Alternatively, don't neglect determining what *not* to do. If you've ever had a truly terrible boss, or simply one that sapped your energy or de-motivated you, consider the matter from the opposite end of the spectrum: what behaviors actually stood in the way of you being the best employee you could have been?

3. **Understand your strengths as well as potential limitations.** Next, you have to consider your current abilities to both implement these good leadership and management practices and avoid the negative ones. This could be harder than you think. A common challenge small business owners face is delegating responsibility. Usually they started their own firms precisely because they valued independence and autonomy. As such, they frequently like "owning" all aspects of an operation, and can find it difficult to relinquish control. You might be one of them. Or you might have other character traits that predispose you to act in one way over another. It's therefore essential that you take a long hard look at your own innate capabilities. Be realistic. Will you have the tendency to micro manage? Will you find it hard to delegate? Will you be able to transfer *authority* as well as responsibility? (A very important distinction—see sidebar.)

4. **Set goals for yourself.** Once you've performed all these analyses, fill out the Management Traits worksheet. Be as specific as possible. You'll end up with a list of do's and don'ts that you can use to guide you as you grow into your new role.

5. **Don't be shy about getting help to achieve those goals.** You can find leadership and management books galore on any bookstore shelf, or by going online. Likewise, you can find well-designed classes and competent coaches —although you should vet the latter carefully before handing over any money—that can help you overcome roadblocks to being the best leader and/or manager you can possibly be.

6. **Balance leadership and management.** Be aware of the danger signals. If you're leading too much, you're going to inevitably see operational or procedural hiccups in your daily operations. If you're leaning too heavily on the management end of the scale, your employees will be de-motivated, won't contribute their best, and you won't be able to think strategically or respond to changing competitive or industry conditions.

Always Give Employees Authority along with Responsibility

Delegating responsibility to employees is a good first step. But it only takes you halfway to your goal of being a good boss. Think of it: you make the wait staff in your café responsible for customer satisfaction. You make it part of their job descriptions, you base their raises on how customers rate them, and you tell them repeatedly that you trust them to ensure that customers never leave the restaurant unhappy. But unless you also give them the *authority* to do such things as discount the price of a meal that was poorly cooked, or offer a free dessert because of the long wait for a table, you are more liable to frustrate your employees than empower them.

worksheet: Management Traits

Use this worksheet to consider your management style and the skills you might need to be the kind of leader you admire.

Management trait you admire or find unhelpful: "I want to…" or "I don't want to.."	How it translates into a specific action to take/not take: "Do's" and "Don't's"	How well suited are you to successfully performing this action?	Skills you need to enhance to achieve this management trait

Communicating Effectively

Once you've isolated those management and leadership qualities that you want to "own"—and created a game plan for acquiring them—it's time to move onto the next major skill you have to master now that you're the boss: communication. And effective communication—whether you are in charge of a team of ten or a single employee—by definition involves a *two-way* conversation.

Sometimes this communication is one-to-one, such as when you have a personal chat with an individual employee. Sometimes it's one-to-many, as when you call a companywide meeting. But in either case, information must flow as easily from your employees to you as it does from you to them.

Once you have information flowing both ways, you must fulfill three key requirements for effective communication: share information as soon as you can; provide clear direction on tasks and assignments; and offer timely, constructive feedback.

■ **Share relevant information early and often.** One thing that will determine your leadership and managerial style is how transparent you choose to be with your employees. You will probably go through some trial and error before you find a balance that works for you. Do you always have to open your books and share the intimate details of your business' finances? Probably not. But if you face some tight times due to losing a major account, it is probably a good idea to brief your employees on how that affects your bottom line. Otherwise, they might worry unduly about their job security as they hear rumors, overhear you talking, or see changes in workflow, which can hurt their productivity and possibly lead them to look for different jobs.

■ **Provide clear direction on tasks and assignments.** You can't just hand off assignments. You have to spend time communicating the specific tasks involved; the goals; the customer or competitive pressures involved; deadlines; and even budgets. The more your employees get a complete view of their work, the more understanding they'll be if a project suddenly is under a time crunch and requires overtime, or if budgets are suddenly tight due to cost overruns.

■ **Offer timely and constructive feedback.** To help new employees grow into their roles, you must give them regular and constructive feedback. Rather than thinking of it as criticism—which could slant what you say in a negative direction—consider it *encouragement*. Employees thrive when you stress what they've done well and make suggestions on how they could do even better.

HIRELearning

Communication in a Web 2.0 World

A booming number of inexpensive or free Web-based tools and applications make communicating and collaborating with employees easier than ever before, especially for small businesses with limited budgets. With tools such as Google Apps (www.google.com/apps/) you and your new team can collaborate on spreadsheets, presentations, and documents, as well as share calendars. Project management software programs such as Basecamp (www.basecamp.com) and Zoho (www.zoho.com) allow you to manage projects, tasks and due dates, and send out email reminders to the team. Inexpensive online communication tools such as Skype (www.skype.com), a telecommunications and instant messaging system, allow you to speak with your employees over the Internet for free or very little. And online meetings hosted by companies such as WebEx (www.webex.com) allow you to conduct virtual meetings with an employee working at home or traveling several time zones away. However, although the Web does offer a multitude of exciting online collaboration applications, don't use them exclusively at the expense of good old-fashioned face-to-face interactions with your employees as well.

Communication Styles Compared

CONSTRUCTIVE	POTENTIALLY DESTRUCTIVE	MICRO-MANAGED
"Thank you for your hard work on the client report; you did a good job in a short time. Next time, include the source data as the client will see that we've done our homework before making recommendations."	"I should never have trusted you with a client report—you left out the source data. I'd never have done that."	"Before you do a client report next time, run it by me each step of the way. Do a summary, then I'll review that; then include the data; and I'll review that; then make the recommendations, and I'll review that. Don't finish anything without checking with me first."
"One of the things customers notice most in a restaurant is their coffee. If it is always hot and the cup never empty, they're more likely to keep coming back. So make sure you keep customers' coffee cups filled and hot and check each table at least once every four minutes."	"I saw a customer with half a cup of coffee. I don't care how busy you are and how many customers you're taking care of."	"I'm going to check each table every four minutes to see if the coffee cups are full."
"Our brand is all about quality. It's what separates us from our competitors. Here are the specific standards that each one of our widgets must meet. Let me know if there's anything keeping you from achieving those standards."	"You screwed up that batch of widgets. I want them perfect!!"	"Because you made that mistake, call me every time you get to this part of the process so I can watch and make sure you don't make that mistake again."
"You didn't greet that last customer. Studies show people buy more if they're greeted within 60 seconds of entering a store. So make sure you say 'Hi, may I help you?' within a minute whenever anyone comes in."	"How could you let that customer just wander around the store without offering assistance? Why aren't you more outgoing?"	"I've got a stopwatch and I'm going to time you each and every time a customer enters the store to make sure you greet them within 60 seconds."

Two-way communication is an acquired skill

Being comfortable providing feedback to your new employee isn't something you should expect to master overnight. The same goes for the idea of seeking—and welcoming—feedback *from employees*. Asking for input from your employee can solve issues that you might not know existed, from scheduling problems to difficulties dealing with customers to ambiguity about a new process.

To facilitate an effective feedback discussion, ask specific, preferably open-ended, questions. Instead of *Are things going okay?* ask *What do you feel is working or not working in your first meetings with new clients?*

The first question is too broad and likely won't invite very specific answers. The second asks for feedback on a specific part of the employee's job. And once you've gotten the feedback, use it. There's nothing more frustrating for an employee than to go out on a limb and venture a suggestion and have nothing come of it. Employees thrive when they know they can have a positive impact. Make sure you act on some of their suggestions and let them know you are taking their advice. That encourages them to keep thinking and contributing.

Motivating and Retaining Employees

Your attitude toward the people you hire determines their attitudes about their jobs. When you trust and empower employees to think about how to solve problems—not just to carry out specific tasks as specifically instructed—you have the potential to unleash impressive amounts of creativity and energy. And, not incidentally, you'll retain the employees you've just spent all this time and money hiring.

Regardless of the management philosophy or model you use, you should be able to motivate and retain good employees if you keep the following basic guidelines in mind:

- **Set standards.** The best way to set standards is by being an example to others. Employees resent being held to higher standards than the boss. Clearly state your expectations, and be consistent. Develop and distribute specific policies and standards regarding the quantity of work expected to be completed, how work processes are to be performed, quality expectations, time off, reimbursements, business travel, and the like. Let employees know the standards by which their performance will be measured and stick to it.

- **Act fairly.** Make sure your standards are reasonable and fair, and that the goals you set are actually achievable. Don't change the rules on the fly—one of the worst things you can do is ask an employee to do things one way today and another way tomorrow.

- **Show respect.** Recognize the unique skills and talents of each person who works with you. Demonstrate to them that you believe they are capable of doing their jobs, even if it takes some time for them to learn. People generally live up to the trust that others show them. Then, as employees gain experience, allow them to make independent judgments and decisions.

- **Listen.** Learn to talk *with* and not just talk *to* your employees. Many employers fail to use their most important resources: their employees' thoughts and ideas. Enlist their suggestions and set goals together. Have problem-solving sessions where employees help devise solutions to your business's problems. Make it clear, however, that decisions usually lie with you. Listen, too, before reprimanding an employee; seek their explanation of why they failed to perform.

- **Offer recognition.** Give rewards. Everyone wants acknowledgement for a job well done. Few things are more deflating than to excel at a task and then have your hard work ignored. What's more, it's just human nature to try harder to please those who appreciate us than those who ignore us. Give credit to all employees who do their job well, with particular rewards for those who perform exceptionally. Give praise quickly and publicly. Often, just a public "thank you" shows that you've noticed their contribution. But specific, tangible rewards—even small ones—reinforce your acknowledgements. Take time to celebrate successes, especially with everyone in the company. It's a morale booster.

Five Ways to Retain Employees

1. **Trust them.** Give your employees responsibility and authority. Show them what has to be done and the standards you want them to meet. Then, let them do their jobs.

2. **Offer them the opportunity to grow.** Although some people might be content to perform the same tasks month after month and year after year, most people would prefer to learn new skills and be given more responsibility as time goes on.

3. **Communicate.** You reduce the chance for misunderstandings and increase the chance of success when everyone on your team knows what's going on. Even short meetings can be helpful and keep you and your employees in sync.

4. **Recognize effort and accomplishment.** Everyone wants to have their hard work acknowledged, even when things don't work out as planned. People thrive when they feel appreciated, and a simple 'thank you,' can make your staff members

feel that they're a valuable, contributing part of your team. Recognition has been shown to be an extremely positive motivator of employee behavior.

5. **Reward accomplishment.** Rewards reinforce behavior. Even small rewards—whether cash, promotions, time off, gifts, something as simple as a candy bar or certificate of achievement—show that you appreciate what they are doing for you and your business and keeps employees wanting to do more.

Other Motivation and Retention Strategies

Recognizing that employee turn-over is costly, especially in a small company, you've got a number of techniques to help you build an atmosphere where employees are more likely to stay and want to do their best for you. Some of them include:

Bonuses, profit sharing

One time-honored way to motivate employees is to create ways for them to benefit financially from your company's long-term financial success. Whether that takes the form of bonuses, profit sharing or the long-term prospect of some equity interest in the business, the possibility of participating in the financial upside of your business can be a powerful motivator.

Sharing goals and sense of purpose

Employees are highly motivated when they, like you, feel their work is accomplishing something important. Even the seemingly most mundane business usually has an important purpose; after all, you're meeting a customer need or desire. For example, you may be running a diaper service—a dirty business indeed. But what you're really doing is providing an important service for new parents at a time when they're the most hassled and concerned about their baby's well-being. Helping your employees to understand the social and personal value in their work makes them more satisfied on a day-to-day basis.

Celebrate

You want your employees to feel like they're part of a team, and they want to feel like they're part of a team. The most successful companies create a sense of partnership and teamwork. One of the best ways to do that is to celebrate successes. Don't just wait for big successes. Taking your staff to lunch to celebrate when a big project is completed makes everyone feel a sense of accomplishment and belonging.

Promote a sense of security

Employees work best when they feel a sense of job security and stability. Certainly there may be times when your finances may be challenged, but if you are continually expressing your worries, they'll be worried too. They may look for other work or just lose their productivity.

Make your employees upwardly mobile

One of the challenges of attracting good workers to a small business and keeping them happily employed there for the long term is that opportunities are by necessity limited.

What you can do, however, is to hire people who you train and nurture to grow as your business grows. By looking ahead and planning carefully, you can invest in well-chosen employees and develop

Code of Employee Ethics

One thing that many organizations have found useful is to generate a "code of employee ethics" that lays out precisely the kind of behavior you expect from employees. This can range from the obvious ("I will respect that company property is for business, not personal, use,") to the more esoteric ("I will treat other employees the way I would like to be treated myself.")

their skills so that as new opportunities arise within your business, you have already groomed valued employees to take on the additional responsibilities.

Mix intrinsic motivators with extrinsic ones

Raises and promotions are important. Employees want—even expect—to be rewarded when they do a good job. But so-called intrinsic motivators in the form of recognition have been proven to be equally important as tangible rewards. Instituting an employee-of-the-month program, recognizing achievements of workers who have gone the extra mile with gift or dinner certificates, or scheduling team-building exercises in which employees are lauded for their individual contributions can do wonders for morale. Indeed, studies have shown that recognition without rewards are more powerful then rewards without recognition. And research has also proven that intermittent positive feedback is the best possible way to motivate people to do better. In other words, getting frequent but not necessarily predictable praise in response to good job performance is a time-honored way to get more out of your employees. Conversely, intermittent *negative feedback* is among the worst behaviors you can engage in, as it fosters insecurity and fear among workers.

Be realistic—and patient

Starting a new job is a stressful endeavor. Some people thrive under pressure. Most don't. Your new hires are meeting new people, learning new processes, and, frequently, new technologies and tools with which to do their jobs. Most will take time to get up to speed. The best way to reduce the learning curve and accelerate productivity is to understand this and make the employees feel safe in a blame-free environment. This means making it okay to make mistakes, even to fail outright, and to treat such events as positive learning experiences.

Of course, you won't be able to keep all people engaged—some will naturally move on—but by investing in new skills as appropriate for your business' long-term goals, you can keep turnover and related costs low.

Lead by example

How you behave, and how you run your business cues employees on the proper way for them to behave as well.

Take ethics. Everyone says they want honest and ethical employees. But how do you successfully instill those qualities in your employees? First (of course) choose as wisely as you can. That's why the vetting part of the hiring process is so critical. But the very best way to ensure ethical employees is to be ethical yourself. If they see you short-changing customers, squeezing suppliers, or cutting corners on quality, they will do the same. Alternatively, if you want them to be engaged and proactive, the very best way to do that is to be engaged and proactive yourself. And try—as much as possible—to keep your mood and energy at high levels. Nothing is more infectious than enthusiasm and excitement, even if it's just for another "ordinary" day at the office.

If you are moody, gossip consistently, fail to show up on time for meetings, your staff will follow in your footsteps. Being the boss means having the responsibility for establishing the standards but it also means living up to those standards. That can be challenging from time to time, but it also calls on you to be your best just as you're asking your employees to be at their best.

Maintain a consistent, positive company culture

When you hired your new employee, you evaluated whether they seemed to be a good fit for your personality and for your company's "culture." If you hired well, your new employee should fit right in. If you prefer a very structured environment, for example, you'll have the best chance of retaining those employees who like strict guidelines. On the other hand, employees like that will not do as well—or stay as long—in a company culture that values independent thinking and judgment.

As you grow, think about the personality or culture of your company and try to maintain an even keel. Just as it is hard to be around an individual with an unstable personality, it's hard to work for a company with an unstable culture. You'll have the highest retention rates in a company with a reliable, consistent company culture.

Performance Review: 30 Days and Beyond

Small businesses rarely do formal performance reviews. But you should institute regular check ins—especially early on—to ensure that everything is on track and that both your goals and your employees' expectations are being met.

- **Check in within 30 days of the hiring date.** Touch base with new hires sooner rather than later so if there are any issues you can catch them immediately. Prior to 30 days, employees might not yet be sufficiently comfortable with the job and their responsibilities to be judged fairly or to give you feedback. At the 30-day point, however, most employees have found their footing, and feel comfortable discussing their performance with you.

- **Give compliments, use criticism sparingly.** Studies have shown that it takes five to nine positive comments to counter the effects of one negative criticism. Even so-called "constructive" criticism has the potential to backfire, as employees may walk away from the review with that criticism ringing in their ears, feeling demotivated. Instead, they should feel that they can earn your approval by doing a good job. You should always be straightforward and honest with employees. But by phrasing feedback as positively as possible you are likely to solicit the best responses from them.

- **Don't spring any surprises.** The performance review—formal or informal—is not the time to surprise new employees with unanticipated issues. You should provide feedback as things

Be careful to document the review

Despite wanting to express things positively, you still need to document any significant issues that have arisen. Although most employment is "at will"—which means either party can discontinue the relationship for any reason at any time—you can reduce the risk of legal liability by carefully documenting the progression of any serious problems.

happen, not save it up for the review. Of course, be careful to NEVER criticize or correct employees in front of others—whether other employees, customers, or visitors.

- **Use the time to ask their advice and suggestions.** At the 30-day mark, employees have been working for you long enough to understand how your business works. Yet they haven't been working long enough to have internalized the corporate culture or processes and feel as though "that's the way it's always done." So the 30-day review is a good opportunity to get a fresh take from a newcomer on how to improve your company. Ask for their specific suggestions and ideas on how to make your processes better, and let them know you want their ideas going forward.

Use the worksheet at the end of this chapter as an outline for your performance reviews, if you choose to conduct them.

Letting Employees Go

Layoffs can be an unfortunate fact of life in the entrepreneurial world. Employers hate them as much as employees do, as layoffs are usually forced upon a business when it's no longer financially possible to keep an worker—or workers—on payroll.

worksheet: Employee Action Plan for Improving Performance

Date: _____

Employee: _____

Management Concern:

_____

_____

_____

_____

Specifics: _____

_____

_____

_____

_____

_____

Plan of Action to Improve Performance: (To be completed by Employee)

Employee Signature: _____

Date: _____

Manager Signature: _____

Date: _____

This review is to be placed in the employee's personnel file.

But sometimes you have to fire employees because they're not performing their jobs in ways that meet your performance standards, are engaging in illegal or unethical behavior, or are endangering other employees. For legal reasons—as previously mentioned—your performance reviews should carefully document the performance-related issues you've encountered with problem employees and show that you gave them the opportunity to correct those issues before terminating them (unless, of course, they're doing something illegal or very dangerous, in which case you'll want to terminate them immediately). But it's important to do this as humanely and decently as possible.

Most companies give terminated employees severance pay, especially when laying someone off. Typically, companies give employees one or two weeks of pay for every year the employee has worked for them. It's good practice to ask the terminated employee to leave immediately even if you pay them for additional weeks worth of work (typically one or two weeks, even if you're firing someone), as it's never a good idea to have a fired, disgruntled employee remain on the job.

Fired and laid off employees will usually be eligible for state unemployment insurance. Find out about this before you meet with them to let them know. Giving them unemployment information helps soften the blow of losing a job.

If you are laying someone off for financial reasons, let them know if they can use you as a reference for other employers. They'll appreciate knowing that you're happy to give them a positive recommendation.

Firing someone is never easy. But as you grow in confidence as a boss, you'll learn that it's sometimes the best thing for both your company and the employee. A bad fit is a bad fit. It's better to identify problems early, give employees a chance to correct them and do a good job. And if that doesn't work, both of you need to be able to move forward to more positive opportunities.

Plan ahead as you continue to grow

Although most small business owners would agree that high employee retention rates are critical, no matter what you do, some good employees will want to move on. Be supportive and respect their personal goals that you might not be able to satisfy. Make it clear you have an "open door" policy that would welcome them should they ever want to return. Stay in touch with them; invite them to company parties. They'll be more likely to return or send other potential employees your way.

Look Who's The Boss

You now have a new title to add to your personal description: "boss." But the term boss doesn't need to have the connotation it once did. You can be a boss your employees respect, a supportive boss your employees turn to for advice and guidance, a fair boss that your employees look to as a role model for their own behavior.

By becoming a boss, you can be one of the people who've created good jobs for others with fair pay, decent working conditions, and a chance for employees to go to work every day in an environment of respect, trust, and honesty. You can give them a chance for personal and professional growth.

By becoming a boss, your employees can help your business grow, take some of the burdens off your lone shoulders, provide you with a sounding board and support. They can reduce your sense of isolation, making your working environment more fun as well as more successful.

By becoming a boss, you're on your way—to a bigger business, a more satisfying work life. And you're helping to create a better economy, too! You've accomplished a lot by taking this important and vital step in the life of your business. You're on your way.

Congratulations, boss!

worksheet: Employee Performance Evaluation

Name _____ Job Title _____

Manager _____

Score the performance in each category a scale of 5 - 1, as follows:

5 = Outstanding

4 = Above Expectations

3 = Meets Expectations

2 = Below Expectations

1 = Continually Fails in this category

Section 1 - Job Duties

Enter key job duties from the job description   **SCORE**

_____   _____

_____   _____

_____   _____

_____   _____

_____   _____

Quality of work _____   _____

Quality of work _____   _____

Section 2 - Personal Performance   **SCORE**

Dependability _____   _____

Attendance & Punctuality _____   _____

Attitude, eagerness to take on more work _____   _____

Flexibility _____   _____

Communication Skills _____   _____

Customer Service _____   _____

Other _____   _____

Section 3—Professional development   SCORE

Training programs _____   _____

Taking on new responsibilities _____   _____

Other professional development _____   _____

_____

_____

Overall Comments

_____

_____

_____

_____

Goals for next review period

1. _____

2. _____

3. _____

Employee Comments

_____

_____

_____

_____

Signatures

Employee _____ Date _____

Manager _____ Date _____

Acknowledgments

Rhonda Abrams and The Planning Shop would like to thank:

Rebecca Gaspar, Managing Editor, who oversaw the entire project of this book from start to finish. It was an extensive project, entailing substantial research and a large and varied staff. Rebecca did it with great grace and talent and kept everything moving.

Mike McClary, Project writer and researcher, who helped create the basic structure and initial information as well as conducting the "Success Story" interviews. He was a pleasure to work with.

Anne Marie Bonneau, Project researcher and copyeditor. Anne Marie, our jill-of-all-trades, easily and effortlessly handled every task from fact-checking, copyediting, proofreading, worksheet creation. She's the newest member of The Planning Shop team. Welcome, Anne Marie!

Alice LaPlante, Project writer and researcher. Alice is our "go-to woman" for great writing, quick turnaround, and all-around fabulous person. We are blessed to have Alice as part of The Planning Shop team.

Diana Russell, Designer. We're so delighted to have Diana back in the Bay Area (out of that Iowa cold) to help us on a regular basis. Talented Diana keeps The Planning Shop look lively and friendly and solves all our layout and design problems.

Eric Powers, Designer, who brought some fresh eyes and new talent to the design of our covers—forcing us to think at least a bit outside our box.

Rosa Whitten, Planning Shop office manager, who keeps everything running while we're busily working on content. Someone has to keep Rhonda organized! She's back from maternity leave, bringing us the newest member of our office team, little Michael Eli.

Sue Raisty-Egami, our digital darling, who helped us find our Success Stories and advised us on our digital transitioning.

The PayCycle team, Jane Willis, Heather Forsythe, Julie McHenry, and Linda Itskovitz. Jane and her PayCycle colleagues were eager backers of this book, providing much valuable information and research material to help us in our efforts. We enjoyed working with you.

The Intuit Payroll team, Nora Denzel, Sharna Brockett, Ken Darrow, Laurie Sheflin, David Shen, and so many others at Intuit who are committed to helping small businesses create jobs and run their businesses more effectively and efficiently. We are so delighted at their enthusiastic adoption of the project to bring this information to many more businesses.

The Success Story subjects, We appreciate these successful small businesses willing to share their stories of struggle and challenge in hiring and growing their businesses: Charles Garrison of Bad Donkey Sub, Salad & Pizza Co.; Ryan Hagel of Motive Marketing; Cindy Hanna of Hanna Design; Mary Keehn of Cyress Grove Chevre (love that Humboldt Fog!); Jennifer McCabe of Team Jenn, and Seth Sternberg of Meebo.com. Thank you all!

Wade Davies, Louise Dupont, and the people of Transcontinental Printing, Transcontinental is not merely our printer; they are our partners and friends. They rushed to meet our deadlines, worked with us to make everything smooth. And we love Wade!

Successful Marketing = Successful Sales
Make More Money!

Successful Marketing: Secrets & Strategies, Deluxe Binder Edition
Includes CD with Complete Excel Marketing Budget Templates

Do you want to grow your business? Are you launching a new business? Do you want to make sure you're getting the most bang for your marketing buck?

You've come to the right place! This much-anticipated book from the creators of the No. 1 business plan guide—*The Successful Business Plan: Secrets & Strategies*—provides entrepreneurs, small-business owners, practicing marketing professionals, and students with everything they need to know to create a successful marketing plan, increase sales, and make more money!

Successful Marketing: Secrets & Strategies includes:

MARKETING ESSENTIALS

• Branding, company identity, and effective marketing messages

• Information on acquiring and retaining customers

• Complete marketing plan template

• Worksheets, checklists, and charts

IN-DEPTH SECTIONS ON THE FULL RANGE OF MARKETING TACTICS AND VEHICLES

• Traditional media—print, radio, TV

• Print collateral—brochures, business cards, direct mail

• Networking, person-to-person, and word-of-mouth marketing

• Other marketing techniques—signs, sampling

UNIQUE FEATURES

• First-ever, exclusive "Affordability Scales"

• "Lingo" gives you must-know marketing terms

• ROI (Return on Investment) calculators

• "Mythbuster" sidebars

COMPLETE ONLINE MARKETING SECTION

• Effective websites

• Search engine optimization and search engine marketing

• Social networking

• Banner, portal & other ads

• Email communications

• Blogs, videos, more!

Available at
www.PlanningShop.com

thePlanningshop

Every successful business starts with a plan.

If you're starting a business, you need to make sure you've accurately assessed your market potential, costs, revenue, competition, legal issues, employee needs, and exit strategy *before* you start investing your (or someone else's) money.

Fortunately, *The Successful Business Plan: Secrets & Strategies* by Rhonda Abrams will show you how to develop a well-crafted, clear, meaningful business plan— step-by-step—that will help ensure you don't end up facing any costly surprises down the road!

Named by *Inc.* and *Forbes* magazines as one of the top ten essential books for small business, *The Successful Business Plan* is the best-selling business plan guide on the market, used in the nation's top business schools and by hundreds of thousands of successful entrepreneurs.

Whether you're seeking funds from outside investors or bankrolling your start-up on your own, *The Successful Business Plan* will be your guide to planning your business in a sound, profitable manner.

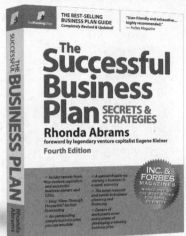

Book features:

• 99 worksheets to help you get started quickly, taking you through every critical section of a successful business plan

• Sample business plan offering guidance on length, style, formatting and language

• The Abrams Method of Flow-Through Financials, which makes easy work of number crunching—even if you're a numbers novice

• Special chapters addressing issues of concern for service, manufacturing, retail, and Internet companies, plus advice on starting a business in a challenging economy

• Nearly 200 real-life insider secrets from top venture capitalists and successful CEOs

"User-friendly and exhaustive...highly recommended."
Forbes Magazine

"There are plenty of decent business plan guides out there, but Abrams' is a cut above the others..."
Inc. Magazine

Available at
www.PlanningShop.com

832084